HISTORICAL DANCES

HISTORICAL DANCES

(Twelfth to Nineteenth Century)

THEIR MANNER OF PERFORMANCE AND THEIR PLACE IN THE SOCIAL LIFE OF THE TIME

Described and Annotated

by

MELUSINE WOOD

Chairman, Historical Dance Branch

With a Foreword

by

CYRIL BEAUMONT, F.R.S.L.

DANCE BOOKS
9 Cecil Court, London WC2

First published 1952.
This edition published 1982.
by Dance Books Ltd.,
9 Cecil Court, London WC2N 4EZ.

© 1982 Imperial Society of Teachers of Dancing

ISBN 0 903102 70 6

CONTENTS

ILLUSTRATIONS

ACKNOWLEDGMENTS

All thanks are due to the Council of the Imperial Society of Teachers of Dancing for publishing this book.

Also to Mr. Cyril Beaumont for much help and encouragement, extending over many years.

I would also like to thank Miss Elsie Palmer for her invaluable help in all matters concerning music, Miss Sylvia Faulkner for reading the proofs, and for her most determined encouragement ; and Mme Anna Ivanova, for valuable help in collecting illustrations.

Thanks are due also to Lt.-Col. H. G. Sotheby, D.S.O., M.V.O., D.L., for permission to reproduce " The Dancing Picture," from Ecton Hall ; to the Libraries' Committee and to Mr. W. J. A. Hahn, F.L.A. (Chief Librarian and Curator) of the South London Art Gallery for permission to reproduce Hogarth's " Study for the Masked Ball at Wanstead Assembly " ; to the Bibliothèque Nationale, Paris, for permission to reproduce two illustrations of the Branle, and a miniature from the MS. " Domenico Cycle " ; and not least, to Miss Margaret Dean Smith and Miss Valerie Prentis for valuable information.

MELUSINE WOOD.

FOREWORD

THERE are many teachers of dancing, but comparatively few include in their *curricula* the teaching of historical dances and, of those who do, how infinitely small is the number who specialize in that phase of dancing alone. The reason is not far to seek. The expert on historical dances needs to be scholar, musician, historian, research worker, detective and linguist—to possess at least a working knowledge of French and, if possible, some acquaintance with Latin, German, Italian, and Spanish in addition.

Miss Melusine Wood, the author of this book, is such a specialist, and, to my personal knowledge, she has devoted a lifetime to the acquisition of material regarding the Historical Dance. Something of the information she has acquired from years of exhaustive study of period dance literature, documents and drawings is made available in the pages that follow.

What more difficult than to ascertain how a particular dance was performed at a particular epoch ! A dancing-master writes for his own generation and, fearing to be thought pedantic, not unnaturally takes much for granted. Even a simple movement such as an eighteenth-century " sink ", or bending of the knees, can become charged with mystery, because the present-day reader does not know to what precise extent the knees were bent, or the correct speed of their fall and rise. Hence, to elucidate such points, contemporary descriptions of a dance in one language must be compared with those in other tongues, that all the available evidence may be considered and weighed. Then there are equally difficult problems of quality and style ; determined partly by a knowledge of the manners and customs of the time ; partly by the kind of costume that was worn and the degree of movement permitted by its cut, weight and length ; and partly by the area in which the dance was done. Such are some of the considerations that have gone to the writing of this book.

The origin and evolution of each dance described is explained, then follow practical instructions—based on documentary evidence—for the performance of the dance, including the relation of steps to bars and beats of the accompanying melody ; and, what is vitally important, each dance is considered in relation to its own historical *milieu* and the period which inspired it. I do not think historical dances have been so presented before, certainly not against so detailed a period background.

Teachers of dancing should be grateful to Miss Wood for her painstaking researches, inspired by her great love of the Historical Dance, which latter has prompted her to make available some of the fruits of her labours for the benefit of dance teachers in general and for the members of the newly-formed Historical Dance Branch of this Society in particular, which organization it is hoped may in the course of time become one of the accepted repositories of such specialized knowledge, to be preserved, added to and passed on from generation to generation to all who wish to learn something of the great dance heritage of the past, as it is mirrored in social activities extending over six centuries of European culture.

CYRIL BEAUMONT.

AUTHOR'S PREFACE

This is not a History of Dancing ; it is a collection of relatively simple dances covering a period of some six hundred years, from the twelfth to the early nineteenth century.

Short notes have been provided for each period to relate the dances to history, especially the history of our own country. The history taught at school generally concerns battles or Acts of Parliament, only rarely does it deal with the lives of ordinary folk like ourselves ; but the history of dancing is about all sorts and conditions of ordinary people, dressed in their best and bent on enjoying themselves.

In a work of limited scope much must be left out, notably the sixteenth-century Italian dances which were the culmination of the Lombard School, and the great figure dances composed by eighteenth-century French masters, all of which demand a higher standard of attainment than we have aimed at here.

The music for old dances always presents a difficulty. The piano is the worst possible instrument on which to reproduce old music, but we must face the fact that it is in general use for all practical purposes to-day. The arrangements given here make no attempt to be academic or old-fashioned, but to provide a straight-forward accompaniment which will help the student to understand the dance. To this end the music for the early dances has been written in clearly-marked four-bar phrases. In modern settings it is usual to write two bars in one, so that a double would be performed in two bars, stepping twice in each bar. An example which should be familiar to everyone is provided by Cecil Sharp's arrangements of the Playford dances.

Something must be said about Style. It is impossible to teach a dance with the written word alone, but in respect of the old dances there are certain principles which may serve to guide us. In all historical periods young people were subject to strict training in deportment from the moment they could walk. This training is a matter on which we are well informed, and we may be sure it influenced their dancing. For the present purpose it is enough to say that no one can go far astray so long as they hold themselves erect without stiffness, and carry their heads high —but not so high that they look down their noses.

Remember that, although we generally approach the old dances with a dramatic performance in view, they were designed in the first place for the enjoyment of the dancer.

Remember also that the essence of well-bred behaviour is the same in all periods. To be simple and unaffected, to be able to wear beautiful costumes without being conscious of them—or of oneself, to avoid any exaggeration, or anything that might inconvenience another person.

It has been difficult to find dances simple enough for an elementary standard. Dancing was never meant to be easy, and our forbears appreciated social graces in proportion as they were difficult to attain. Methods of teaching varied, but on one point the masters of all periods agreed. If you want to dance you must practise.

Historical Notes

12th to 14th Century

TWELFTH AND THIRTEENTH CENTURIES

In the early Middle Ages the most cultured courts in Europe were those of the Provençal nobles. Provence then was of greater extent than it is now ; and instead of forming part of France, it was attached to the Spanish kingdom of Aragon.

The ancient Greeks had a settlement at Marseilles, and later Provence became a Roman Province. To this inheritance of Greek and Roman traditions the Provençal nobles in the eleventh and twelfth centuries added much that they learned from Hispano-Moorish culture. The result was a race of fighting, singing poets whom we call the Troubadors. When they were not fighting, the Troubadors used to gather in some garden, or in a woodland glade, to discuss matters of interest, and to exchange songs and verses ; dancing must have been part of the entertainment, because most of their songs are written in dance rhythms. Their ladies presided over these assemblies, and acted as judges.

Most social gatherings took place out of doors in the Middle Ages, because houses—even castles—had only small windows, and tended to be dark and smoky.

Costume was reasonable and comfortable in the twelfth and thirteenth centuries. ·The robes do not appear to have been made of heavy material, and ladies were able to tuck them up into their girdles for activities like dancing. There were no exaggerated head-dresses : for festive occasions both men and women wore wreaths of sweet-scented flowers such as roses, violets and jasmine. Shoes were beautifully made in soft leather, following the natural shape of the foot. The Lady in " The Romance of the Rose " had footwear of this kind :

> " Upon her well-shaped feet I ween,
> Most carefully-made boots she'll set,
> Whereof the joints so well are met,
> That, not a plait or crease will show,
> But on her legs they'd seem to grow."

" The Romance of the Rose," LXXIII. 14248. Trans.: F. S. Ellis. The Temple Classics.

Until the time of the Troubadors one dance had served for gentle and simple folk alike. This was the Carole. A Carole means a dance for which the music is sung, usually by the dancers themselves ; it was always a linked dance, and it had two distinct forms.

First there was the Farandole[1] (see Example I), inherited from the Greeks, and still the national dance of Provence. A Farandole is a line of dancers in single file, each holding the hand of the next. The leader takes them where he

[1] See Figure 2.

(or she) will, either through the streets of the town, or meandering about its square; wandering round the paths in a garden, or tracing figures on the lawn. A Farandole might run madly, or walk sedately; it was essentially an out-of-door dance.

The second form of the Carole was the Round, or Branle[1] (see Example II), in which the dancers hold hands in a circle. Dancers in a closed circle cannot trace figures like the free-moving Farandole, but they can move to left or right, and also vary the rhythm of their steps. French writers tell us that Ronde and Branle are almost synonymous words. The name Branle comes from the characteristic movement to left and right alternately. The French verb " branler " means " to sway." Later, we will find English Rounds which are not Branles. Although more compact than the Farandole, the Branle was also an outdoor dance.

These linked dances are impersonal. It makes no difference whether the dancers are all girls, all boys, or mixed couples. There is no room in a Carole for individual virtuosity; these dances demand perfect team work.

Pictorial evidence suggests that the Farandole was more common in Italy and the Branles in France. Provence used both forms.

The impersonal Carole did not satisfy the Troubadors, whose social system centred on the duty owed by each gentleman to the one lady of his choice; they evolved a dance called Estampie, which was performed by one gentleman with one lady; or, more rarely, by one gentleman with two ladies.[2] Two or three voices were no substitute for the full chorus of the Carole, so the music of the Estampie was instrumental.

These simple innovations produced tremendous results. The two or three dancers no longer moved crabwise, but were free to dance forward and back, or to weave patterns among themselves; the way was open for all future developments of dance form.

The musical results were no less significant; because when secular instrumental music ceased to be merely an accompaniment for the voice, it increased in interest and importance until it won complete independence.

The steps of the Estampie were those used in the Suite of Common Branles. We know this because there is a MS[3] containing music for three Estampies, and this music can be used equally well for the Common Branles. (See Examples II, III, IV.) Nevertheless, even musically, there was a difference between the two dances. A Branle has a music-unit, allied to a dance-unit, which are repeated for as long as the dancers please. The Estampie has several such units, arranged according to a set pattern, and having a definite beginning and end. Therefore, when we use Estampie music for the Branles, we take only the first unit and repeat it instead of playing the whole composition.

The Estampies in MS. Harley 978 are straightforward adaptations of the Common Branles; but we find in many twelfth and thirteenth century songs that units might be taken from more than one Branle to build an Estampie. Varying combinations of Branle Double with Branle Simple were most usual.

The Estampie must have been mainly an open-air dance, like the Carole; but it had the compact form associated with indoor dances. It is reasonable to imagine the assembled company ranged in a semi-circle on either side of the

[1] See Figure 3.   [2] See Figure 5.   [3] British Museum MS. Harley 978.

presiding lady, leaving a limited central space within which singing, dancing or disputation would take place.

The Albigensian Crusade, which began in 1208, wiped out Provençal Society, and those Troubadors who escaped with their lives took refuge in various European Courts ; they were welcome everywhere on account of their songs and their dances, and nowhere more than in England. The English Angevin Kings had always been in close touch with Provence ; Henry II and Henry III both married Provençal princesses. It was during the reign of Henry III that the MS. now known as Harley 978 was written at Reading Abbey.

An inhuman campaign resulting in the massacre of thousands of women and children does not, at first sight, appear to have much connection with dancing ; but in fact the Albigensian Crusade had important and beneficial results on the development of the Art ; it offers an example of the close relation between dance history and the history of nations.

Instead of remaining a local Provençal dance, the Estampie was transplanted by fugitive Troubadors to Italy, Sicily, Germany, France and England, and its future development was subject to different influences in each country. Only in England no development took place, and we have the curious phenomenon of pure Thirteenth Century dances surviving into the Sixteenth Century.

THE FOURTEENTH CENTURY

Progress is seldom continuous. After the activity of the Twelfth and Thirteenth Centuries there was a lull for the next hundred years ; but beneath the surface growth continued unseen, preparing to burst into flower in the Fifteenth Century. With one notable exception no new dance appeared. Occasional references indicate that the Estampie was still used ; but no hint is given of the influences that were re-shaping it in various countries.

At this point it may be useful to explain briefly what these influences were. Whilst allowing for the elusive " Spirit of the Age " we find that dance form is dictated by two entirely practical considerations ; first, the size and shape of the dancing place ; and second, the costume worn by the dancers.

In England, Germany, and the northern parts of France, the centre of activity was always the Hall ; whether in Palace, Castle, Manor House or on a smaller scale in the houses of rich merchants. These great Halls were all built on the same plan. On entering, one found oneself in a passage ; this was really a part of the Hall cut off by a wooden screen. Doors in the screen gave entrance to the body of the Hall. The screen did not go up to the roof ; a gallery was built over it, running back over the passage, and here the musicians played for dancing. In the centre of the Hall was the hearth, with a vent in the roof over it to carry off the smoke. From the Fourteenth Century onwards it became more usual to build a large hooded fireplace at the side of the hall, with a proper chimney. At the far end of the Hall was the dais, a raised platform on which the master of the house, with his family and honoured guests, could sit somewhat removed from the general company. There are many of these Halls still to be seen in England ; notably the Hall at Penshurst in Kent, which retains the central hearth.

Trestle tables were set up at dinner time, but after the meal they were taken down and stacked at the lower end of the Hall near the screen, leaving only the benches round the sides.

There was now ample space for dancing. The Rounds could group themselves naturally about a central hearth, and they retained their popularity until the Seventeenth Century. With the hearth moved to the side, and the centre of the Hall free, there was a tendency to develop a processional form—dancers moving up the Hall, and then making a turn to go back to where the dance started. Due reverence was paid to the great ones on the dais, who were honoured with bow and courtesy at the beginning and end of the dance. This custom continued into the Eighteenth Century when the dais was always called " the top of the room," and the bow and courtesy were known as " honouring the presence."

Although the family sat apart on the dais, life was shared with the whole household. All met for dinner, and if dancing followed all joined in. The superior people might dance an Estampie by themselves, but Round or Farandole needed the co-operation of all. The division does not seem to have been into gentle and simple so much as into old and young. Doubtless the simple folk learnt the Estampies in this way, and then it was but a short step to the village green ; only so can we account for the fact that they were preserved by our country folk, to be returned to court in the Sixteenth Century as English Country Dances.

The second ruling factor was costume. During the Fourteenth Century, French costume became progressively more voluminous and heavy for the ladies, and even the men wore long robes. To balance their robes the ladies' head dresses spread out in horns, and other fantastic shapes.[1] This made a processional dance almost inevitable, because the bulky garments could not be tucked up into a girdle as they had been in the Thirteenth Century ; they must either be left to trail, or carried over one arm. Any active movement was discouraged ; a quick turn was impossible.

England followed French fashions in dress.

In the south, and especially in Italy, domestic architecture was based on the Roman villa. Instead of the great Hall there were rooms built round a central Court. In a room—even a large room—gatherings were more intimate in character. The gentlefolk, not mixing with their household, created a more sophisticated style. The limited space available encouraged the growth of figure dancing.

Italian costume in the Fourteenth Century was full and weighty, but it never ran to the length of a French robe, and whereas in the Fifteenth Century French costume showed even greater extravagance, the Italians moved towards the refinement and grace of Renaissance styles. Therefore Italian dancing was free to develop a greater vivacity as well as variety of form.

The one new dance produced by the Fourteenth Century came from Germany. The Germans called it the Trotto, and so at first did the Italians, but later they changed the name to Saltarello Todesco, or " German Saltarello." Elsewhere

[1] See Figure 4.

14

the Trotto was generally known as the Almain or Allemande, which means simply " German dance."

The Almain is a Branle de Bourgogne danced forward, and showing minor variations after the manner of an Estampie.

The Branle de Bourgogne, fourth in Arbeau's suite of Common Branles, was omitted in dealing with the Thirteenth Century because contemporary music made no provision for it ; but it may well have existed at the time as a separate dance. The step is simple and universal ; it is common to peasant dancers throughout the world to-day.

The first detailed description of this Branle comes, like the others, from Arbeau's " Orchésographie " ; it is a form of Branle Double, but danced more lightly and quickly. It is danced in a circle.

Bar.	Beat.	
1	1	Step with the left foot, turning slightly to the left.
	2	
2	1	Step with the right foot, near the left.
	2	
3	1	Step with the left again.
	2	
4	1	Hop on the left, and swing the right forward and across the left with
	2	a straight knee.

Arbeau does not mention the hop on the fourth bar, but it is implied ; because in describing the movements of raising the foot (pied en l'air and grue) he says there is a spring on to the supporting foot. In this case, seeing one is standing on the supporting foot already, the spring must be a hop.

The same steps are repeated to the right, beginning with the right foot ; and of course, observing the usual rule in Branle, to make the steps to the left larger than those to the right in order to move round the circle.

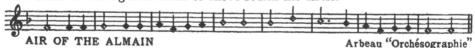

AIR OF THE ALMAIN   Arbeau "Orchésographie"

The Almain described by Arbeau uses the same step, but made in a forward direction by couples dancing in procession.

Bar.	Beat.	
1	1	Step forward with the left.
	2	
2	1	Step forward with the right.
	2	
3	1	Step forward with the left.
	2	
4	1	Hop on left and raise right forward.
	2	

15

This Double is characteristic of the Almain, and it is therefore reasonable to call it the " Almain Double."

There is contemporary evidence for the introduction of the Almain into England. In 1338 King Edward III paid a visit to the Emperor at Coblenz ; it was part of a political manœuvre, and the English king was fêted royally. Some years later, Froissart mentions " the German dance " lately introduced by Sir John Chandos.

As in France, the steps of the Almain were not recorded until the Sixteenth Century. The cycle of Elizabethan MSS. in which the steps of the Estampie are found, contains many Almains. These fall into two classes, of which the first is headed by the " Old Almain," and the second by the " New Almain." The music for the " Old Almain " is in even eight-bar phrases, whilst the phrasing for the " New Almain " and others of its kind is uneven, comprising both eight- and twelve-bar phrases.

The dance called the " Old Almain " may be the original dance received from Germany, because it is similar in form to an Estampie Double but with certain significant variations.

To dance the " Old Almain " partners must face each other and take both hands. In this position they change places with two Simples and a Double, beginning with the left foot and moving round to the left. They repeat the two Simples and a Double, but beginning with the right foot and moving round to the right to regain their original places. As they finish the last Double, the gentleman must release his partner's right hand, and they open out to finish standing side by side, and shoulder to shoulder, with the joined hands raised forward to shoulder level. This first part of the dance needs sixteen bars in duple time.

For the second part of the dance they move forward, and both beginning with the left foot, they make four Almain Doubles, at the end of which they take both hands to begin again. This second part also needs sixteen bars in duple time. Whilst there are many good Almain airs belonging to the Sixteenth Century, the earlier periods present difficulties ; however, the " Old Almain " could be danced to any folk song falling into two strains of sixteen bars each.

Comparing the " Old Almain " with the Estampie Double, it appears that the four Almain Doubles forward correspond to the Double forward Double back repeated, of the Estampie Double. The two Simples and a Double form the normal variation. It should be noted that in the " Old Almain " the order is reversed, and the variation comes first. The distinguishing features of the Almain are these :

(1) The music is in duple time.
(2) The foundation of the dance is the characteristic Almain Double, though ordinary Doubles are used in the variation sections.
(3) From pictures we learn the forward raised position of the hands. This, again, is characteristic of the Almain, marking it off from the Basse Dance and the Pavane in which the hands are not raised.
(4) Pictures also teach us that at the end of the Almain Double it is the knee rather than the foot that is raised ; the lower part of the leg is allowed to hang naturally instead of being stuck out stiffly.

16

Fig. I. ALMAIN EARLY 16TH CENTURY

From " The Dancing Picture," the property of Colonel Sotheby, Ecton Hall, Northants

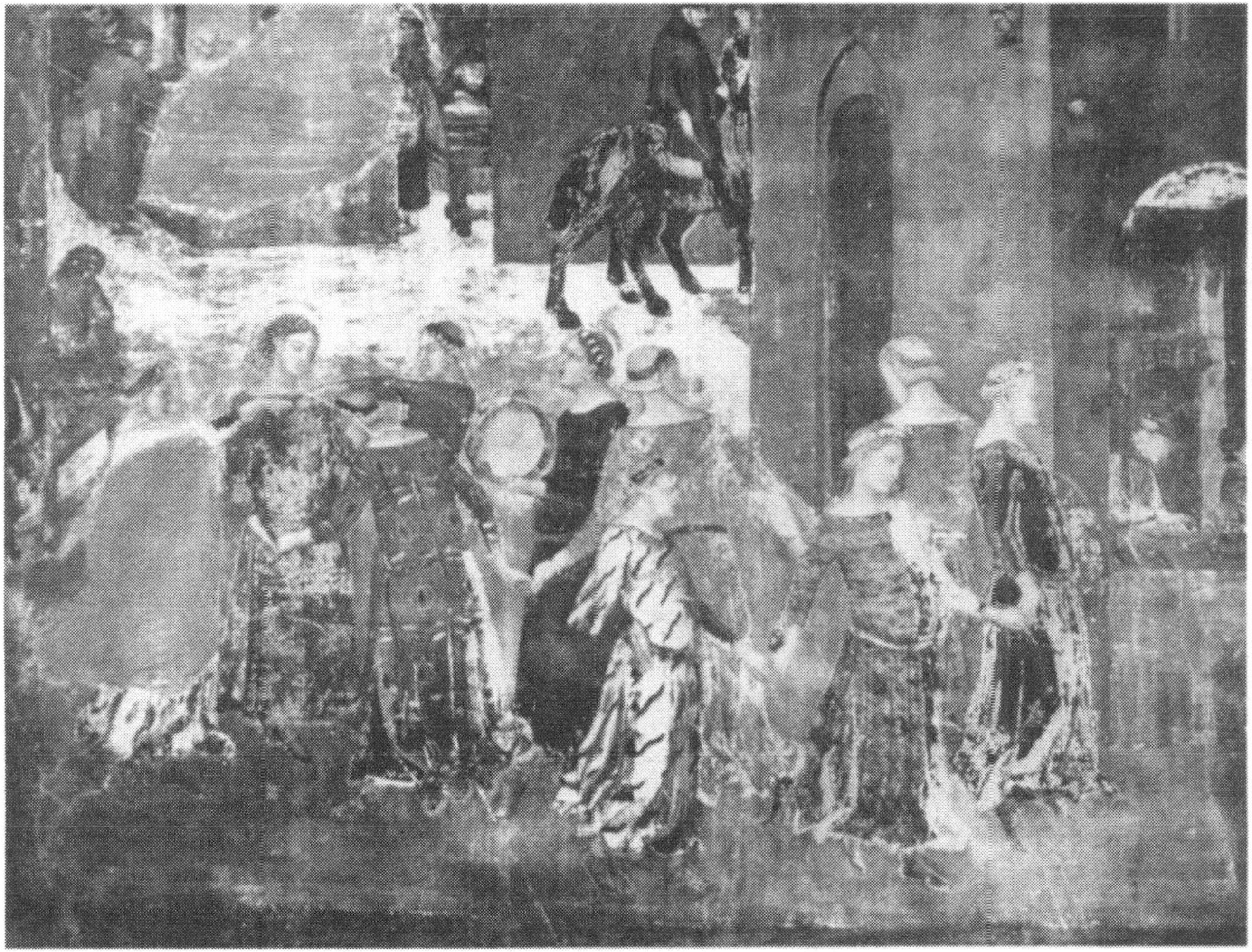

Fig. II. FARANDOLE, CIRCA 1337

Detail from the Fresco, " Good Government," by Ambrozio Lorenzetti

(5) The Almain is the first processional recorded amongst social dances. The Farandole was in single file, the Estampie for two or three dancing alone. In the Sixteenth Century, Von Wedel—attending a ball at Queen Elizabeth's court—thought a German dance was in progress because the dancers arranged themselves in column one couple behind the other, and he was surprised to find it was a Pavane; evidently the processional form was distinctively German in his eyes.

It may well be asked why a Branle de Bourgogne danced in the form of an Estampie should be a German dance? History offers a reasonable explanation. When Beatrix of Burgundy went to Germany in 1156 to marry the Emperor Frederick Barbarossa, she took with her a Trouvère, Guiot de Provins. Here we have a Burgundian and a Provençal influence entering Germany at the same moment. It is generally held that Guiot founded the Minnesinger tradition in Germany. The Minnesinger were the German counterpart of the Troubadors. If, therefore, Guiot was responsible for the introduction of Provençal music into Germany, it is almost certain he introduced the Provençal dances also; he may have made an Estampie from the Burgundian Branle as a compliment to his patroness. In the course of two hundred years such a dance would be moulded by native German influences until it was accepted as a German dance. This is guess work, and cannot be proved as yet; but it is certain that during the Fourteenth Century a dance spread throughout Europe from Germany, and this dance combined the general characteristics of the Estampie and the Branle de Bourgogne.

Fourteenth-century French miniatures are almost unanimous in depicting Rounds. French musical evidence bears out the idea that the Branles were still the favourite French dance, but now they were more often the Branles Coupés; that is to say combinations of units from the three dances of the Common Suite in varying proportions. This resulted in highly uneven phrasing of the music, and exercised great influence on the growth of the Basse Dance which was destined to dominate the Fifteenth Century.

In Italy the Estampie was used in the Fourteenth Century, and with it the Saltarello; there is musical evidence for the use of the Trotto (or Almain).

In Spain the situation was more complex, but we know that the Alta was the Spanish counterpart of the Saltarello, and there are traces of Estampie form in later Spanish dances.

The "Alexander" romance in the Bodleian Library (c. 1340) shows a miniature of a round dance, and also a Farandole, both evidently current in England at the time; and as it was explained above, the Almain became known here some time before 1350.

We must turn to the Fifteenth Century to see the result of the changes which had been maturing in the various European countries.

Dances

12th to 14th Centuries

EXAMPLE I

THE FARANDOLE.

If you want to dance a Farandole you must all take hands in a line. The one at the end of the line who has her left hand free is the leader ; the last dancer will have her right hand free. Any number can dance. If the numbers are uneven everyone in turn has a chance to lead ; but even numbers mean that only the first of every pair can do so. All holding hands, face towards the leader, and you are ready to begin. Only two steps are needed—skipping step when the line is moving freely, and walking step for the figures. Nowadays French Folk Dancers sometimes use fancy steps, but they were added in the last century by dancing masters.

To begin with the line winds in and out, and round about where ever the leader chooses ; but when she thinks it is time to make a change she may start one or other of the figures.

The most popular figure is called " Threading the Needle " because in it the dancers all pass under an arch (as in Oranges and Lemons). Long ago, artists were fond of painting this figure, so we know it must be very old.

When the leader thinks it is time to Thread the Needle she steps round to face the second dancer ; they both stop, and hold up their arms to form an arch. The third dancer lets go the second dancer's hand, the line changes to walking step, and all follow the third dancer through the arch. The last on the line, who has her right hand free, takes the left hand of the original leader, who follows through the arch by turning under her own right arm ; she is now second-last on the line, and the original second dancer is the last. They may keep on Threading the Needle until the original leader comes to the top again ; but one of the others may decide to introduce a different figure.

Another old figure is called " L'Escargot " or " The Snail " because it is like a snail curling itself into its shell. The leader coils the line into a spiral, and when she reaches the centre she makes an arch by turning the second dancer under her arm. As nobody releases hands, the others must all follow the second dancer through this arch until the line is straight again.

There is a third figure in which everyone stops, and they all hold up their arms to make arches. The leader goes under the arch made by number two and number three ; she comes out between three and four, and so on, drawing the line after her. Of course each arch disappears in turn, until once more the line is straight.

Example I   FARANDÒLE
Old French. From Bladé "Poésies Populaires de Gascogne"
Arranged by Elsie Palmer

SUMER IS ICUMEN IN
Round. For the Carole in Farandole Form

British Museum MS. Harley 978

Su - mer is i - cu - men in   Loud now sing cuc - cu.   Grow-eth

seed and blow-eth mead and spring the woods a - new.   Sing   cuc - cu

Ewe now call - eth af - ter lamb, and af - ter calf the cow.

Bul-lock start-eth Buck now ver-teth Mer - ry sing cuc - cu   Cuc -

- cu,   cuc - cu   Well singst thou cuc - cu   Mer-ry, mer-ry sing cuc - cu.

$\overset{2}{V}$ = *Second voice enters*
$\overset{3}{V}$ = *Third voice enters*

19

It often happened that several lines were dancing at the same time; and when two lines met they would release hands and thread through each other, passing right and left alternately until the lines were clear and each was free to go on its own way again. As you probably know already, this figure was called the Hey; it forms part of many dances and it even became an independent dance itself; but whenever we find a Hey we remember the Farandole.

EXAMPLE II (A)

To Dance the Common Branles.

Any number may dance the Common Branles, and they must take hands in a ring. Although these dances are so simple they can look really beautiful when they are danced carefully; by stepping exactly on the beat; and by making the turns to left and right all together, not jerkily, but with an easy movement in time to the music.

Branle Double.

Branle Double consists of a Double to the left, and a Double to the right; and because the dancers want to move round the circle the Double to the right is made with small steps, almost in place.

Bar.	Beat.		
1	1	Step with the left.	
	2		
	3		
2	1	Step with the right.	Double to left.
	2		
	3		In making these steps turn
3	1	Step with the left.	towards the left, so you
	2		walk forward rather than
	3		sideways.
4	1	Close the right, but without	
	2	putting weight on it.	
	3		
5	1	Step with the right.	
	2		
	3		
6	1	Step with the left.	Double to right.
	2		
	3		In making these steps turn
7	1	Step with the right.	towards the right, and
	2		make very small steps,
	3		almost in place.
8	1	Close the left without putting	
	2	weight on it.	
	3		

Example II

ESTAMPIE DOUBLE
For Branle Double use first sixteen bars only

Air from British Museum MS. Harley 978
following the transcription by the Rev. Dom Anselm Hughes O.S.B.
in "Early English Harmony" Plainsong & Mediæval Music Society

Arranged by Elsie Palmer

EXAMPLE II (B)

To Dance the Estampie Double.

Partners stand side by side, holding inside hands without raising the arms at all. Both use the same feet. There is no evidence to show whether the steps were made on the toes ; pictures suggest that they were not.

Bar.	Beat.		
1	1	Step forward with the left foot.	
	2		
	3		
2	1	Step forward with the right foot.	
	2		
	3		
3	1	Step forward with the left foot.	Double forward.
	2		
	3		
4	1	Close the right foot to 1st position.	
	2		
	3		
5	1	Step back with the right foot.	
	2		
	3		
6	1	Step back with the left foot.	
	2		
	3		
7	1	Step back with the right foot.	Double back.
	2		
	3		
8	1	Close left to 1st position.	
	2		
	3		
9	1	Step forward with the left foot.	
	2		
	3		
10	1	Step forward with the right foot.	
	2		
	3		
11	1	Step forward with the left foot.	Double forward.
	2		
	3		
12	1	Close right to 1st position.	
	2		
	3		

Bar.	Beat.		
13	1	Step back with the right foot.	
	2		
	3		
14	1	Step back with the left foot.	
	2		
	3		Double back.
15	1	Step back with the right foot.	
	2		
	3		
16	1	Close the left to 1st position.	
	2		
	3		

Second Part :

1	1	Step with left to 2nd position.	
	2		
	3		Simple left.
2	1	Close right to 1st position.	
	2		
	3		
3	1	Step with right to 2nd position.	
	2		
	3		Simple right.
4	1	Close left to 1st position.	
	2		
	3		
5	1	Step forward with the left foot.	
	2		
	3		
6	1	Step forward with the right-foot.	
	2		
	3		
7	1	Step forward with the left foot.	Double forward.
	2		
	3		
8	1	Close right to 1st position.	
	2		
	3		
9	1	Step with right to 2nd position.	
	2		
	3		Simple to right.
10	1	Close left to 1st position.	
	2		
	3		

23

Bar.	*Beat.*		
11	1	Step with the left to 2nd position.	
	2		
	3		
12	1	Close right to 1st position.	Simple to left.
	2		
	3		
13	1	Step back with the right.	
	2		
	3		
14	1	Step back with the left.	
	2		
	3		Double back.
15	1	Step back with the right.	
	2		
	3		
16	1	Close left to 1st position.	
	2		
	3		

The third part also has sixteen bars, and they are danced exactly as in the first part.

Therefore it can be seen that Estampie Double consists of two units of Branle Double danced forward and back ; and divided by sixteen bars of variation in which the double forward and double back are interrupted by two Simples to the side (English Country Dance " Setting ").

This dance was known in Queen Elizabeth's time as a Country Dance, and it was danced to an air called " Turkeyloney." The steps of " Turkeyloney " are preserved in several late Elizabethan MSS., and without this evidence we would not know that the two Simples were made to the side.

EXAMPLE III (A)

BRANLE SIMPLE.

Branle Simple consists of a Double to the left and a Simple to the right.

Bar.	*Beat.*		
1	1	Step with the left.	
	2		
	3		
2	1	Step with the right.	Double to left.
	2		
	3		In making these steps turn
3	1	Step with the left.	towards the left so you
	2		walk forward rather than
	3		sideways.
4	1	Close the right, but without	
	2	putting weight on it.	
	3		

24

Bar.	Beat.		
5	1	Step with the right.	
	2		Simple to right.
	3		
6	1	Close the left without putting	In making this step turn
	2	weight on it.	towards the right.
	3		

EXAMPLE III (B)

To Dance Estampie Simple.

The Estampie Simple does not follow exactly the same pattern as Estampie Double ; though in this case also the sequence of the Branle is interrupted by Simples to the side. Instead of forming a middle section, they come at the end of each part like a cadence. Now two Simples need four bars of music, but Branle Simple is written in six-bar phrases. Apparently the Provençal musicians felt the difference between four and six bars would be too great, so they wrote five bars for the Simples, that is to say two bars for the Simple to the left and three for the Simple to the right.

Bar.	Beat.		
		Partners stand as for Estampie Double, and use the same feet.	
1	1	Step forward with the left foot.	
	2		
	3		
2	1	Step forward with the right foot.	
	2		
	3		
3	1	Step forward with the left foot.	Double forward.
	2		
	3		
4	1	Close the right to 1st position.	
	2		
	3		
5	1	Step back with the right.	
	2		
	3		Simple back.
6	1	Close left to 1st position.	
	2		
	3		

25

7	1	Step forward with the left foot.	
	2		
	3		
8	1	Step forward with the right foot.	
	2		
	3		
9	1	Step forward with the left foot.	Double forward.
	2		
	3		
10	1	Close right to 1st position.	
	2		
	3		
11	1	Step back with the right foot.	
	2		
	3		
12	1	Close left to 1st position.	Simple back.
	2		
	3		
13	1	Step forward with the left foot.	
	2		
	3		
14	1	Step forward with the right foot.	
	2		
	3		
15	1	Step forward with the left foot.	Double forward.
	2		
	3		
16	1	Close right to 1st position.	
	2		
	3		
17	1	Step back with the right foot.	
	2		
	3		
18	1	Close left to 1st position.	Simple back.
	2		
	3		
19	1	Step with left to 2nd position.	
	2		
	3		
20	1	Close right to 1st position.	Simple to left.
	2		
	3		

Bar. Beat.

21	1	Step with right to 2nd position.	
	2		
	3		
22	1		
	2		Slow Simple to right.
	3		
23	1	Close left slowly to 1st position.	
	2		
	3		

The slow Simple to the right is made more easily if the step to the right is made on the toes. For the second bar, close the left, also on the toes. For the third bar lower both heels. Performed in this way the slow Simple to the right becomes the Italian Ripresa, or Reprise, and is linked to the slow Simple backwards which was also called Reprise.

From the end of the twenty-third bar, the whole Estampie Simple is repeated.

EXAMPLE IV (A)

BRANLE GAI.

Branle Gai is different, because it moves to the left all the time ; because the steps are sprung ; and because they are made on the beat instead of one to each bar as they were in the first two Branles.

Bar. Beat.

1	1	Spring on to the left foot, raising the right forward.
	2	Spring on to the right foot, raising the left forward.
	3	Spring on to the left foot, raising the right forward.
2	1	Spring on to the right foot, raising the left forward.
	2	Pause.
	3	
3	1	Spring on to the left foot, raising the right forward.
	2	Spring on to the right foot, raising the left forward.
	3	Spring on to the left foot, raising the right forward.
4	1	Spring on to the right foot, raising the left forward.
	2	Pause.
	3	

And so on, always beginning with the left foot because you are always moving to the left.

The springs should be small, because the object is to cover the ground quickly, not to jump high. It is helpful to give a good push forward with the foot that is raised, and to let the weight pass forward with it.

Example III

ESTAMPIE SIMPLE
for Branle Simple use only the first twelve bars

From British Museum MS. Harley 978

Arranged by Elsie Palmer

M.M. $\quad$ = 88

28

Example IV

ESTAMPIE GAI
for Branle Gai use the first sixteen bars only

From British Museum MS. Harley 978

First Part

M.M. ♩. = 80

Arranged by Elsie Palmer

Second Part

Example V

BRANLE COUPÉ
"En ma Dame"

Arranged by Elsie Palmer

EXAMPLE IV (B)

THE ESTAMPIE GAI.

Partners stand side by side, holding inside hands without raising the arms at all. They use the same feet.

Bar. Beat.

1	1	Spring on to the left foot, pushing the right forward.
	2	Spring on to the right foot, pushing the left forward.
	3	Spring on to the left foot, pushing the right forward.
2	1	Hop on the left foot.
	2 ⎫	
	3 ⎬ Pause.	
3	1	Spring on to the right foot, pushing the left forward.
	2	Spring on to the left foot, pushing the right forward.
	3	Spring on to the right foot, pushing the left forward.
4	1	Hop on the right foot.
	2 ⎫	
	3 ⎬ Pause.	

Continue in this way until the end of the thirty-second bar, moving straight forward round the dancing place. If possible finish at the back facing forward.

Bar. Beat.

Second part :

1	1	Step forward with the left foot.	
	2		
	3		Simple forward.
2	1	Close the right to 1st position.	
	2		
	3		
3	1	Step forward with the right foot.	
	2		
	3		Simple forward.
4	1	Close the left to 1st position.	
	2		
	3		
5	1	Step forward with the left foot.	
	2		
	3		
6	1	Step forward with the right foot.	
	2		
	3		
7	1	Step forward with the left foot.	Double forward.
	2		
	3		
8	1	Close the right to 1st position.	
	2		
	3		

Bar. Beat.

9	1	Step back with the right foot.	
	2		
	3		
10	1	Close the left to 1st position.	Simple back.
	2		
	3		

11	1	Step back with the left foot.	
	2		
	3		
12	1	Close the right to 1st position.	Simple back.
	2		
	3		

13	1	Step back with the right foot.	
	2		
	3		
14	1	Step back with the left foot.	
	2		
	3		
15	1	Step back with the right foot.	Double back.
	2		
	3		
16	1	Close the left to 1st position.	
	2		
	3	Release hands.	

In making the next step they must face each other and take right hands, in order to change places with the following Simples and Doubles :

Bar. Beat.

17	1	Step forward with the left foot.	
	2		
	3		
18	1	Close the right to 1st position.	Simple forward.
	2		
	3		

19	1	Step forward with the right foot.	
	2		
	3		
20	1	Close the left to 1st position.	Simple forward.
	2		
	3		

32

Bar. Beat.

21	1	Step forward with the left foot.	
	2		
	3		
22	1	Step forward with the right foot.	
	2		
	3		Double forward.
23	1	Step forward with the left foot.	
	2		
	3		
24	1	Close the right to 1st position.	
	2		
	3	Release hands.	

In closing the right to 1st position in bar 24 they must each make a half-turn to the right in order to take left hands and return to their places.

Bar. Beat.

25	1	Step forward with the right foot.	
	2		
	3		Simple forward.
26	1	Close the left to 1st position.	
	2		
	3		
27	1	Step forward with the left foot.	
	2		
	3		Simple forward.
28	1	Close the right to 1st position.	
	2		
	3		
29	1	Step forward with the right foot.	
	2		
	3		
30	1	Step forward with the left foot.	
	2		
	3		Double forward.
31	1	Step forward with the right foot.	
	2		
	3		
32	1	Close the left to 1st position.	
	2		
	3	Release hands.	

The man must make a half turn left, so they face forward and take inside hands as at the beginning of this part.

33

Bar.	Beat.		
33	1	Step forward with the left foot.	
	2		
	3		Simple forward.
34	1	Close the right to 1st position.	
	2		
	3		
35	1	Step forward with the right foot.	
	2		
	3		Simple forward.
36	1	Close the left to 1st position.	
	2		
	3		
37	1	Step forward with the left foot.	
	2		
	3		
38	1	Step forward with the right foot.	
	2		
	3		
39	1	Step forward with the left foot.	Double forward.
	2		
	3		
40	1	Close the right to 1st position.	
	2		
	3		
41	1	Step back with the right foot.	
	2		
	3		Simple back.
42	1	Close the left to 1st position.	
	2		
	3		
43	1	Step back with the left foot.	
	2		
	3		Simple back.
44	1	Close the right to 1st position.	
	2		
	3		

34

Bar.	Beat.		
45	1	Step back with the right foot.	
	2		
	3		
46	1	Step back with the left foot.	
	2		
	3		
47	1	Step back with the right foot.	Double back.
	2		
	3		
48	1	Close the left to 1st position.	
	2		
	3		

It must be stressed that whereas in Estampie Double and Estampie Simple there are grounds for supposing the reconstruction to be correct, in Estampie Gai it is pure conjecture. However, the conjecture is based on :

(1) The indications given in the music.
(2) Consideration of the forms taken by the first two dances of this suite.
(3) Attention to the Elizabethan dances of the same type, but so far not represented in the Thirteenth Century examples.

Musically the dance is divided into two parts, of which the first consists entirely of Branle Gai danced forward.

The second part of the music is sub-divided into three sections of sixteen bars each. A dance-unit of two Simples and a Double performed six times is indicated.

Several alternative readings of this second part suggest themselves, any of which may be correct :

(1) The steps may be danced forward all the time. This disregards the sub-division into three parts.
(2) Following more closely the composition of the previous dances we might have :

Simple left. Simple right. Double forward.
Simple right. Simple left. Double back.

This unit :

(a) Might be repeated for each sixteen bars.
(b) It might be used for the middle sub-section only ; dancing forward and
    back for the first and last sub-sections after the manner of Estampie
    Double.
(c) It may be used as in the chosen interpretation, based on an Elizabethan
    dance called " Tinternel," which was linked with " Turkeyloney,"
    but which has not so far been represented in the Thirteenth Century
    examples. " Tinternel " has plain Doubles forward and back,
    varied by two Simples and a Double taking hands and going round.
    This is satisfactory in that it accounts for the dance-unit of two
    Simples and a Double ; and also for the sub-division into three equal
    parts.

35

Branles Coupés.

Besides the Common Branles there were others, called Branles Coupés; these were composed by using steps or whole sections, taken from the Common Suite. Many of the examples given by Arbeau are complicated, but in the earlier period they were simple enough.

.The example given here illustrates the principle in its most elementary form. The song, "En ma Dame," has a six-bar phrase followed by one of eight bars, then two six-bar phrases to complete the music-unit. The dancer must make the following steps :

Double left, Simple right, once.

Double left, Double right, once.

Double left, Simple right, twice.

FIG. III.   CAROLE, 14TH CENTURY
From Guillaume de Marchaut. "Remède de Fortune"
(Paris : Bib. Nat. fonds fr., 1586)

FIG. IV. BRANLE, 15TH CENTURY, FRENCH
" La Danse devant Amour "
(Paris : Bib. Nat. fonds fr., 1696, Fol. 1)

Historical Notes

15th Century

THE FIFTEENTH CENTURY

From the Fifteenth Century onwards, the dance historian is no longer fitting together fragments of evidence. Both in France and in Italy books were written by dancing masters, and from them we learn the wide divergence of style in the two countries.

England had nothing to offer at this time ; our contribution would be made later. The main centres of interest were France and Italy ; but Spain must not be left out of account. The Spanish people have always shown a particular genius for dancing, and their influence is apt to appear in unexpected places.

The Fifteenth Century was the Age of the Basse Dance. It is usual to define Basse Dance as a dance performed with gliding steps close to the ground, as opposed to the Danse Haute or Alta which was sprung. This explanation takes no account of contemporary evidence. It is open to question whether Alta means high in the sense of elevation ; the Spanish word conveys more a sense of dignity and importance, as we mean to do in speaking of a Royal Highness.

The earliest French Basse Dances use springing steps. It is true that in the final form the springing " Pas de Brébant " was only used at the end ; but in Italy the Saltarello which corresponded to " Pas de Brébant " was quite as likely to come at the beginning of the dance, and isolated groups of Saltarello steps not infrequently occur in the middle.

According to contemporary evidence, the Basse Dance was so called because it was of lowly origin. Thus Toulouze, in " L'Art et Instruction de bien Dancer," says it is called Basse Dance " pour ce que quand on la danse on va en pays sans soy demener le plus gracieusement qu'on peult " (because when one dances it one goes in country fashion without bearing oneself as graciously as one might). The Burgundian MS. reads " Paix " (peace) for " pays," but it is clear in either case that the dancer of Basse Dance was not expected to put on courtly airs.

The Italians linked Basse Dance with Piva (though at opposite ends of the scale ; Piva being the country Measure proper to shepherds and the like).

Something has been said already about the influences shaping social dances, but costume and environment do not supply the whole picture. In France and England, in the Netherlands and Germany, life had much in common with our own times. The Mediæval world was nearing its end. Strange and horrible new weapons of war were coming into use. Instead of the Long Bow, from which the goose-feathered cloth-yard shaft was loosed by a balanced and beautiful movement of the archer, cross-bowmen wound their metal bows by mechanical means to shoot the iron quarrel. Even worse were the cannon fired with gun-powder. These engines of the devil made mounted knights in shining armour obsolete ; to many it must have seemed that the future held no place for gentlemen if wars were to be fought by smoke-blackened soldiery. In consequence, the ceremonial and decorative aspects of chivalry were developed in a high degree and the spirit was lost.

With this background of stark fact, Society became ever more artificial. Instead of the Twelfth-century knights and ladies, flower-wreathed, dancing to the sound of their own voices on shady lawns, we find ladies with plucked eyebrows and painted faces, the length of their robes balanced by the height of their head-dresses, trailing through palace halls. Their flowers were of jewels and enamel ; their music strident trumpets.

Although the Hall remained the centre of activity, there is some evidence to suggest that dancing sometimes took place in the upper galleries where the ladies had their apartments. In England the habit of strewing floors with rushes and sweet herbs persisted into the Sixteenth Century, but Fifteenth Century pictures show airy and elegant interiors with arches rising from slender pillars, and floors tiled with black and white squares.

Everything in social life became more formal, more systematic, more obedient to fixed rules. The Basse Dance reflected these tendencies faithfully, and must be regarded as the characteristic dance of the period ; nevertheless the Rounds or Branles are most commonly represented in contemporary miniatures. These show a welter of pointed head-dresses and floating veils, with heavy robes either looped over, or tucked under, one arm. It looks most uncomfortable for all parties (Fig. 4). How much easier the steady progress up and down the Hall or Gallery with train flowing, which was possible in a Basse Dance !

The final form of Fifteenth-century French Basse Dance, as set out in Toulouze and the Burgundian MS., was governed by precise rules. These rules are apt to appear meaningless, but they are nearly all traceable to the original Branles. One example must suffice : In Basse Dance the first of any group of steps moving forward must be made with the left foot ; and in moving back the step must be made with the right foot. In a Branle danced in a circle, to move to the left was " forward," and one began naturally with the left foot. Moving to the right was " back " and began with the right foot.

Since the dancers knew with which foot to begin, and how the steps were made, in describing a dance it was only necessary to note the names of the steps in their order. Steps were represented by their initial letter.

R. A capital R stood for Révérence, the initial bow and curtsey.
b. A small b denoted Branle, a movement of courtesy associated with the Révérence, and replacing it in the body of the dance.
c. Sometimes the Branle was called Congé, in which case it was indicated by a small c.
ss. Meant two Simples.

38

d. Stood for one Double, ddd for three Doubles.

r. A small r meant a Reprise, rrr three Reprises.

For details of the steps see page 44 *et seq.*

The only difficulty in a Basse Dance of this kind was to remember the order of the steps. To make this easier, the steps were arranged in groups called Measures, which in turn were subject to fixed rules. There were usually from three to five Measures, of which two or more might alternate, or they might all be different.

French Basse Dance did not crystallise into its fixed form until the Fifteenth Century was far advanced. The first French dances whose steps have been recorded were used for a Fête at Nancy in 1445. This brings us back to English History, because the festivities were in honour of Margaret of Anjou, who had been married by proxy to King Henry VI, and was on her way to join him in England. It is therefore at least probable that these dances became known in England.

The Nancy Basse Dances are interesting because they show the process of change from Estampies and Branles Coupés to Basse Dance proper ; they do not obey the fixed rules described later, but the beginning of the form is apparent.

The usual Simples, Doubles and Reprises were used, with the Branle here called Congé ; but in addition there were springing steps (Saults) ; Levées (Arbeau's Pied-en-lair) ; and Pas Menus. Since the Pas Menus were always in groups of three, it is reasonably sure they were made one to the minim beat (three to the bar) as opposed to ordinary steps which were one to the dotted semibreve or bar. It is usual to halve the values of notes for modern use, so the Pas Menus are made on crotchet beats now. Passi Minimi, steps made on the minim beat, were used in Italy in the Sixteenth Century.

A feature which looked back, rather than forward, was the use of Simples in groups of three, requiring a six-bar phrase in the music. These three Simples often open the dance, without any preliminary Révérence, from which we may argue that Simples were made in the Fifteenth Century manner with a bow. In the English Salisbury MS. Révérence is commonly replaced by ss, or b. Since the left foot must be ready to begin the first Double forward, the first Simple of three begins with the right.

The example chosen here from the Nancy collection in the " Basse Danse de Bourgogne " (Example VI, p. 46). This dance is only irregular in that it uses groups of three Simples. With the three Simples it can be written in Branle form ; but by omitting the first Simple in every group of three, the dance can be written in Measures and becomes regular according to the later rules.

The Nancy Basse Dances tell us that even as late as 1445 the Basse Dance had not crystallised into its final form ; consequently these dances have much more life and interest than the later ones.

ITALY IN THE FIFTEENTH CENTURY

Whilst the Mediæval social structure was dying in France, Italy was rising on the full tide of the Renaissance. Nothing in life was fixed or certain ; the small states into which the country was divided were often at war with each other, or suffering civil strife within ; but the re-discovery of the ancient Greek learning brought new ideas of order, proportion and beauty. Many of the world's masterpieces of painting and sculpture were created at this time, although they were in constant danger of destruction. The Italians might respect Art, but the same could not be said for the foreign mercenaries brought in to fight Italian interstate wars.

The pendulum was swinging to its fullest extent. At one end were battle, murder, and pillage ; at the other, the fixed determination to make life beautiful in every aspect. Most lives were poised somewhere between the two extremes.

Only in Ferrara, under the Marquis Leonello d'Este (1441-1450), learning and the arts had free play uninterrupted by war. Leonello was a rare spirit, a connoisseur in life ; his first concern was to make the University famous throughout Europe ; he beautified his palaces and gardens ; he encouraged goldsmiths and craftsmen of all kinds as well as artists and sculptors ; he surrounded himself with a court renowned for wit and learning, for beauty and virtue. For all this, Leonello was no prig, and the lighter forms of amusement were practised provided they conformed to the æsthetic ideal. Ferrara was destined to become the nursery of " the Lombard style of dancing."

Greek Art was never static ; it had always a sense of movement based on the balanced perfection of the human body, therefore it is not surprising that the art of dancing had great prominence in the Italian Renaissance. Amongst the artists who flocked to Leonello's court was the " worthy and respected knight, messer Domenico of Piacenza."

Domenico must have made his name already, because the well-known writer Antonio Cornazzano tells us that he was Domenico's pupil in Piacenza ; but it is as Domenico of Ferrara that he is more generally known. Domenico does not seem to have written anything himself, but a number of MSS. exist which were written by his pupils : some commentators have been puzzled by the degree of unanimity shown by these MSS. but surely nothing else was to be expected if the pupils recorded their master's teaching faithfully. The best pupil was Guglielmo Ebreo (William the Jew), who himself became a composer of dances.

Domenico was no reckless innovator ; rather he took all the material that came to hand and moulded it into a new form. He was aware of the state of dancing in many lands ; thus he said that the Italian Saltarello was the same as the Pas de Brébant and the Spanish Alta. Italian Quadernaria Measure was " Saltarello Todesco " (German Saltarello). In certain dances there is mention of a Portuguese Reprise.

We have seen that in the Fourteenth Century Italians were dancing Estampies, Saltarelli, and the German Trotto. According to Antonio Cornazzano, the favourite dances in the Fifteenth Century were Basse Dances and Saltarelli. Unfortunately there is nothing to show whether Domenico was responsible for the Italian Basse Dance, or if it was already in use when he began his work. Domenico was working at Ferrara in the fourteen forties—that is to say, about the time that the French Basse Dance was taking shape so there would be nothing improbable in the supposition that Italian Basse Dance was regulated by him.

French Basse Dance carries within itself proof of its origin in the Estampie and the Branles. Italian Basse Dance derives as surely from the Estampie and the Farandole. The simplest form of Italian Basse Dance is in file, a Farandole in which the dancers have released hands, and move in file, one behind another. The file may consist of two dancers only, or of any number up to " as many as will." In the simplest form of the dance they move up the room, face about, and dance back to the bottom, facing about to regain their original positions.

In the next form rudimentary figures appear ; the dancers may exchange places, pass and re-pass, meet and part again. Our example (Example VIII) belongs to this class ; it is called Zinevra, after one of Leonello's sisters. Zinevra belongs to the darker side of the Italian Renaissance ; she was married at fifteen to one of the Malatesta, and he poisoned her when she was only twenty-one ; such things would be far from her mind when she danced her own Basse Dance at Leonello's court.

In the end, the Basse Dances were entirely figured ; danced by three or four weaving in and out, dancing the figure of eight round one another, or joining in the Hey.

Domenico's fertile brain did not stop at Basse Dance ; he created a new form called Balli (dances) or Balletti (little dances). These were uniformly figure dances, and their keynote was variety. There was variety in the number of dancers employed, and in the balance of the sexes. In one case a single lady dances with five gentlemen ; her partner, and four others who try to take her away from him.

The music for a Basse Dance was played from a given Tenor, and one Tenor could serve for any Basse Dance, but a Ballo has its own music specially composed, and could not be danced to any other. Domenico's system was based on four Measures. The French used this word to " Measure " the number of steps in a section of their Basse Dance ; Domenico's Measure was musical and represented a more complicated version of the old Branle punctum with its accompanying step. It would take too long to attempt a complete description of the Lombard system of dancing ; it must suffice to say that there were four Measures, so related that each was to be one-sixth slower than the one before.

(1) Piva was the original peasant measure in triple time ; it went so quickly that the only possible step was a Double unadorned.

(2) Saltarello, said to resemble Pas de Brébant, therefore to be compared with the Branle Gai. Also in triple time.

(3) Quadernaria, otherwise called German Saltarello, was the Almain. Quadernaria was a musical term used in Italy in the Fourteenth Century to denote a semibreve containing four minims instead of the normal two, or three. Therefore Quadernaria was in Common time.

(4) The slowest measure was Basse Dance. Like Piva, the basic step was the Double, but performed slowly it has to be adorned with certain graces.

The graces and ornaments used with Basse Dance and Saltarello are described on page 61, but even when these had been mastered Domenico had not finished with his pupils ; they must be prepared not only to change quickly and neatly from one measure to another, but to fit the step of one to the music of another.

Basse Dance and Piva were easily interchangeable because Piva music was exactly the half of Basse Dance. It was harder to dance the triple time measures in Quadernaria.

Certain exercises were recommended. If you want to know whether you are proficient, you should let the musician vary the measure, trying to put you out, and you must follow him so quickly that you are always in time. Contrarywise, you may dance out of time and let the musician try to play in time with you, but you must never be caught dancing in time. This is a far cry from the placid French Mediæval systems.

Domenico's definition of dancing shows how his mind worked. He says that dancing reveals the sweet harmony created in our hearts by music ; for this sweetness and harmony, being imprisoned within us, struggle to get out, and can only issue forth as beautiful movement.

The pupil was expected to know that a Double consisted of three steps, and a pause as the foot is closed. In the Lombard style the pause is all important. The dancer must stop as if he had seen Medusa's head and been turned to stone ; he must start again as a frightened falcon spreads its wings. Aiere, the controlled rise and fall of the instep, is also described vividly : " The dancer must rise and fall gently, as a gondola rises and falls on the little waves of the lagoon. He must dance with feeling and imagination, or he will fail." It seems unlikely that Domenico ever counted " one-two-three-and . . ." in his lessons. To understand him, the pupil had to be acquainted with classical mythology, and must have observed the flight of birds and such things as the way of a boat on the water. One might suppose this to have been natural to an educated Italian of the Renaissance, yet in one manuscript we meet the heartfelt cry of exasperation : " For pity's sake open your mind, and use the brain that God has given you."

A great deal remains to be said about the Lombard style of dancing, but there is no space for it here.

Besides the Basse Dance " Zinevra " two Balli have been described :

" Prexonera " for two, combining Basse Dance with Piva and Saltarello (Example IX) ; and

" Anello " for four, strongly suggestive of an English Country Dance (Example X).

Dances

15th Century

FRENCH

STEPS USED IN FRENCH BASSE DANCE

(1) Révérence, or Bow and Curtsy.

(a) *Bow.*—When a Mediæval man wished to show respect he knelt on one knee. This was not good for the knees of his hose, and soon it became usual to take the foot back and bend the knee without actually letting it touch the ground. For the bow before dancing it is enough to take the left foot back to a small fourth position, and bend the knee half way to the ground. Keep the weight over the front foot

(b) *Curtsy.*—The lady was always expected to kneel on both knees in showing respect ; but for less important occasions, and for dancing, she can make the same movement as that described above for the man. The Révérence was written in dance notation with a capital R ; it was made in the time of a four-bar phrase.

Bar.	Beat.	
1	1	Take the left foot back to fourth position, keeping the weight over the
	2	front foot.
	3	
2	1	Bend right knee and relax the left, but keep head and shoulders up
	2	and look at the person to whom you bow.
	3	
3	1	Straighten the knees again.
	2	
	3	
4	1	Close the left foot to first position.
	2	
	3	

It was usual for the man to wear a hat whilst dancing. He should take it off with his left hand before beginning the bow, and hold it close beside him with the inside turned in towards himself. The hat should be put on again as the foot is closed in the fourth bar ; the man then offers his right hand to his partner, who places her left hand in his. The hands should be kept low ; if they are raised at all it should not be above the elbow.

(2) THE BRANLE.

This step was called Branle because in making it the dancers sway from one foot to the other. It is a movement of courtesy, and it comes from the two Simples to the side that were made in the Estampie ; in this case, however, there is no step to the side, the feet are kept in the first position. Branle was written with a small b in notation. Like the Révérence it needs four bars of music. You must rise on your toes on the last beat of the previous bar.

Bar.	Beat.	
4	1	
	2	
	3	Rise on the toes.
1	1	Drop on to the outside foot, relaxing the inside knee, and making a slight turn away from your partner.
	2	
	3	Rise on the toes and face forward again.
2	1	Lower both heels together.
	2	
	3	Rise on the toes.
3	1	Drop on to the outside foot, relaxing the inside knee as before ; but this time look back at partner over your shoulder.
	2	
	3	Rise on the toes and face forward again.
4	1	Lower both heels together.
	2	
	3	

(3) THE SIMPLES.

Basse Dance music was written in even four-bar phrases, therefore Simples, which only need two bars, were made in pairs to fill out the phrase. The Simple was written with a small s, and two were written where two Simples were needed : ss.

By the Fifteenth Century steps were more ornamental, and the two Simples were made in this way :

Bar.	Beat.	
1	1	Step forward with the left foot, bowing slightly to the left.
	2	
	3	
2	1	Close the right foot to first position, rising on the toes.
	2	
	3	
3	1	Step forward with the right foot on the toes.
	2	
	3	
4	1	Close the left foot to first position and lower the heels.
	2	
	3	

This movement is rather like a bow, and in some MSS. they wrote ss instead of R before the dance.

44

(4) THE DOUBLE.

The Double is almost exactly like the old one, but the three steps forward must be made lightly, on the toes.

Double was written with a small d, and they put as many of them as there were Doubles to be danced.

The Double needed four bars.

Bar. Beat.

1	1	Step forward with the left foot on the toes, keeping the weight forward over the foot.
	2	
	3	
2	1	Step forward with the right foot in the same way.
	2	
	3	
3	1	Step forward with the left foot in the same way.
	2	
	3	
4	1	Close the right foot to first position and lower the heels.
	2	
	3	

If another double followed, it would begin with the right foot.

(5) THE REPRISE.

The Reprise in French Basse Dance was one Simple made backwards, but in the time of four bars. It was made with a little bow in opposition to the foot in front. The four movements should be made so smoothly that they seem to be one.

Reprise was written with a small r to distinguish it from the Révérence. Reprises were always uneven in number, and the first one always began with the right foot.

Bar. Beat.

1	1	Take a small step back with the right foot.
	2	
	3	
2	1	Make a little bow to the left side.
	2	
	3	
3	1	Raise the body again.
	2	
	3	
4	1	Bring the left foot back to first position.
	2	
	3	

The next Reprise would be made in the same way, but beginning with the left foot, and the third would be exactly like the first one.

EXAMPLE VI

EARLY FRENCH BASSE DANCE. 1445. (Nancy.)
LA BASSE DANSE DE BOURGOGNE

Bar.	Beat.		
A. 1	1	Step forward with the right foot,	
	2	bowing slightly to the right.	
	3		Simple R.
2	1	Straighten slowly, closing left foot to	
	2	first position.	
	3		
3	1	Step forward with the left foot,	
	2	bowing to the left.	
	3		Simple L.
4	1	Straighten slowly, closing the right	
	2	foot to first position.	
	3		
5	1	Step straight forward with the right	
	2	foot on the toes.	
	3		Simple R.
6	1	Close the left to first position and	
	2	lower the heels.	
	3		
B. 1	1	Step forward with the left, lightly	
	2	on the toes.	
	3		
2	1	Step forward with the right, lightly	
	2	on the toes.	
	3		Double L.
3	1	Step forward with the left, lightly	
	2	on the toes.	
	3		
4	1	Close the right to first position,	
	2	lowering the heels.	
	3		
5	1	Step forward with the right, lightly,	
	2	on the toes.	
	3		
6	1	Step forward with the left, lightly,	
	2	on the toes.	
	3		
7	1	Step forward with the right, lightly,	Double R.
	2	on the toes.	
	3		
8	1	Close the left to first position,	
	2	lowering the heels.	
	3		

B. 2.

Bar.	Beat.		
1	1	Step forward with the left, lightly,	
	2	on the toes.	
	3		
2	1	Step forward with the right, lightly,	
	2	on the toes.	
	3		Double L.
3	1	Step forward with the left, lightly,	
	2	on the toes.	
	3		
4	1	Close the right to first position,	
	2	lowering the heels.	
	3		
5	1	Step forward with the right, lightly,	
	2	on the toes.	
	3		
6	1	Step forward with the left, lightly,	
	2	on the toes.	
	3		Double R.
7	1	Step forward with the right, lightly,	
	2	on the toes.	
	3		
8	1	Close the left to first position,	
	2	lowering the heels.	
	3		
A. 1	1	Step forward with the left, lightly,	
	2	on the toes.	
	3		
2	1	Step forward with the right, lightly,	
	2	on the toes.	
	3		Double L.
3	1	Step forward with the left, lightly,	
	2	on the toes.	
	3		
4	1	Close the right to first position,	
	2	lowering the heels.	
	3		
5	1	Step with the right to second posi-	
	2	tion, on the toes.	
	3		Simple to R.
6	1	Close the left to first position, and	
	2	lower the heels.	
	3		

47

B. 2.

Bar. Beat.

I	I	Step with the right to second posi-	
	2	tion, on the toes.	
	3		
2	I	Close the left to first position, lower	Simple to R.
	2	the heels.	
	3		

3	I	Step with the right to second pos-	
	2	tion, on the toes.	
	3		
4	I	Close the left to first position, lower	Simple to R.
	2	the heels.	
	3		

5	I	Step back with the right to third	
	2	position, bowing to the left.	
	3		
6	I	Transfer weight to the right foot.	
	2		
	3		Reprise R.
7	I	Close the left to first position.	
	2		
	3		
8	I	Straighten the body.	
	2		
	3		

C. I	I	Step back with the left to fourth	
	2	position, bowing to the right.	
	3		
2	I	Transfer weight to the left foot.	
	2		
	3		Reprise L.
3	I	Close the right foot to first position.	
	2		
	3		
4	I	Straighten the body.	
	2		
	3		

Bar.	Beat.		
C. 5	1	Step back with the right foot to	
	2	third position, bowing to the left.	
	3		
6	1	Transfer weight to the right foot.	
	2		
	3		Reprise R.
7	1	Close the left to first position.	
	2		
	3		
8	1	Straighten the body.	
	2		
	3		
9	1	Step with left to second position,	
	2	turning left.	
	3		Simple L.
10	1	Close right to first position and face	
	2	forward.	
	3		
11	1	Step with the right to second posi-	
	2	tion, turning right.	
	3		Simple R.
12	1	Close left to first position, and face	
	2	forward.	
	3		

Congé (= Branle).

The Second Part of the Dance.

Bar.	Beat.		
A. 1	1	Step forward with the right foot,	
	2	bowing to the right.	
	3		Simple R.
2	1	Straighten slowly, closing left foot	
	2	to first position.	
	3		
3	1	Step forward with the left foot,	
	2	bowing to the left.	
	3		Simple L.
4	1	Straighten slowly, closing the right	
	2	to first position.	
	3		
5	1	Step straight forward with the right	
	2	on the toes.	
	3		Simple R.
6	1	Close the left to first position, and	
	2	lower the heels.	
	3		

49

A. 2.

Bar. *Beat.*

1	1	Step forward with the left, lightly,	
	2	on the toes.	
	3		
2	1	Step forward with the right, lightly,	
	2	on the toes.	
	3		
3	1	Step forward with the left, lightly,	Double L.
	2	on the toes.	
	3		
4	1	Close the right to first position, and	
	2	lower the heels.	
	3		
5	1	Step forward with the left foot,	
	2	bowing to the left.	
	3		Simple L.
6	1	Straighten slowly, closing right foot	
	2	to first position.	
	3		

B. 2.

1	1	Step forward with the right foot,	
	2	bowing to the right.	
	3		Simple R.
2	1	Straighten slowly, closing left foot	
	2	to first position.	
	3		
3	1	Step straight forward with the left	
	2	foot, on the toes.	
	3		Simple L.
4	1	Close the right to first position, and	
	2	lower the heels.	
	3		
5	1	Step back with the right to third	
	2	position, bowing to the left.	
	3		
6	1	Transfer weight to the right foot.	
	2		
	3		Reprise R.
7	1	Close the left to first position.	
	2		
	3		
8	1	Straighten the body.	
	2		
	3		

50

Bar.	Beat.		
C. 1	1 2	Step back with the left to fourth position, bowing to the right.	
	3		
2	1	Transfer weight to the left foot.	
	2		
	3		
3	1	Close the right to first position.	Reprise L.
	2		
	3		
4	1	Straighten the body.	
	2		
	3		

5	1 2	Step back with the right foot to third position, bowing to the left.	
	3		
6	1	Transfer weight to the right foot.	
	2		
	3		
7	1	Close the left foot to first position.	Reprise R.
	2		
	3		
8	1	Straighten the body.	
	2		
	3		

9	1 2	Step with the left foot to second position, turning left.		
	3		Simple L.	
10	1 2	Close the right to first position and face forward..		Congé (= Branle).
	3			
11	1 2	Step with the right to second posi- tion, turning right.		
	3		Simple R.	
12	1 2	Close the left to first position, and face forward.		
	3			

Example VI

Music for the
BASSE DANSE DE BOURGOGNE

Arrangement of "Cils a qui je suis Ami"   Arranged by Elsie Palmer

Example VII

Tenor "Engoulême" arranged for
BASSE DANSE "LA DAME"

Introduction
M.M. ♩. = 60

A

Arranged by Elsie Palmer

EXAMPLE VII

French Basse Dance : "La Dame"
From the Salisbury MS. Late Fifteenth Century

First Measure.

Bar.	Beat.		
I	I	Step forward with the left, bowing	
	2	slightly to the left.	
	3		Simple L.
2	I	Close the right foot to first position,	
	2	raising the body.	
	3		
3	I	Step forward with the right foot,	
	2	bowing slightly to the right	
	3		Simple R.
4	I	Close the left foot to first position,	
	2	raising the body.	
	3		
A. I	I	Step forward with the left foot,	
	2	bowing slightly to the left.	
	3		Simple L.
2	I	Close the right foot to first position,	
	2	raising the body.	
	3		
3	I	Step straight forward with the right,	
	2	on the toes.	
	3		Simple R.
4	I	Close the left to first position, lower-	
	2	ing the heels.	
	3		
5	I	Step forward with the left foot, on	
	2	the toes.	
	3		
6	I	Step forward with the right foot, on	
	2	the toes.	
	3		
7	I	Step forward with the left foot, on	Double L.
	2	the toes.	
	3		
8	I	Close the right foot to first position,	
	2	lowering the heels.	
	3		

55

9	1	Step forward with the right foot,	
	2	on the toes.	
	3		
10	1	Step forward with the left foot,	
	2	on the toes.	
	3		Double R.
11	1	Step forward with the right foot,	
	2	on the toes.	
	3		
12	1	Close the left foot to first position,	
	2	lowering the heels.	
	3		

13	1	Step forward with the left foot,	
	2	on the toes.	
	3		
14	1	Step forward with the right foot,	
	2	on the toes.	
	3		Double L.
15	1	Step forward with the left foot,	
	2	on the toes.	
	3		
16	1	Close the right foot to first position,	
	2	lowering the heels.	
	3		

A. 2.

1	1	Take a small step back with the	
	2	right foot.	
	3		
2	1	Make a little bow to the left side.	
	2		
	3		
3	1	Raise the body again.	Reprise R.
	2		
	3		
4	1	Bring the left foot back to first	
	2	position.	
	3		

Bar.	Beat.		
5	1	Take a small step back with the	
	2	left foot.	
	3		
6	1	Make a little bow to the right side.	
	2		
	3		Reprise L.
7	1	Raise the body again.	
	2		
	3		
8	1	Bring the right foot back to first	
	2	position.	
	3		
9	1	Take a small step back with the	
	2	right foot.	
	3		
10	1	Make a little bow to the left side.	
	2		
	3		Reprise R.
11	1	Raise the body again.	
	2		
	3		
12	1	Bring the left foot back to first	
	2	position.	
	3	Rise on the toes.	
13	1	Drop on to the outside foot, relaxing the inside knee,	
	2	and making a slight turn away from your partner.	
	3	Rise on the toes, and face forward again.	
14	1	Lower both heels together.	
	2		
	3	Rise on the toes.	Branle.
15	1	Drop on to the outside foot, relaxing the inside knee,	
	2	but this time look back at partner over your shoulder.	
	3	Rise on the toes and face forward again.	
16	1	Lower both heels together.	
	2		
	3		

SECOND MEASURE

Bar.	Beat.		
B. 1	1	Step forward with the left foot,	
	2	bowing slightly to the left.	
	3		Simple L.
2	1	Close the right foot to first position,	
	2	raising the body.	
	3		

57

3	1	Step straight forward with the right	
	2	foot, on the toes.	
	3		Simple R.
4	1	Close the left to first position, lower-	
	2	ing the heels.	
	3		

5	1	Step forward with the left foot, on	
	2	the toes.	
	3		
6	1	Step forward with the right foot, on	
	2	the toes.	
	3		Double L.
7	1	Step forward with the left foot, on	
	2	the toes.	
	3		
8	1	Close the right foot to first position,	
	2	lowering the heels.	
	3		

9	1	Take a small step back with the	
	2	right foot.	
	3		
10	1	Make a little bow to the left side.	
	2		
	3		
11	1	Raise the body again.	Reprise R.
	2		
	3		
12	1	Bring the left foot back to first	
	2	position.	
	3	Rise on the toes.	

13	1	Drop on to the outside foot, relaxing the inside knee,	
	2	making a slight turn away from your partner.	
	3	Rise on the toes and face forward again.	
14	1	Lower both heels together.	
	2		
	3	Rise on the toes.	
15	1	Drop on to the outside foot, relaxing the inside knee,	Branle.
	2	but this time look back at partner over your shoulder.	
	3	Rise on the toes, and face forward again.	
16	1	Lower both heels together.	
	2		
	3		

58

THIRD MEASURE.

A. 3.

Bar. *Beat.*

I	I	Step forward with the left foot,	⎫	
	2	bowing slightly to the left.		
	3			Simple L.
2	I	Close the right foot to first position,		
	2	raising the body.		
	3		⎭	

3	I	Step straight forward with the	⎫	
	2	right foot on the toes.		
	3			Simple R.
4	I	Close the left foot to first position,		
	2	and lower the heels.		
	3		⎭	

5	I	Step forward with the left foot,	⎫	
	2	on the toes.		
	3			
6	I	Step forward with the right foot,		
	2	on the toes.		
	3			Double L.
7	I	Step forward with the left foot, on		
	2	the toes.		
	3			
8	I	Close the right foot to first position,		
	2	and lower the heels.		
	3		⎭	

9	I	Step forward with the right foot,	⎫	
	2	on the toes.		
	3			
I0	I	Step forward with the left foot, on		
	2	the toes.		
	3			Double R.
II	I	Step forward with the right foot, on		
	2	the toes.		
	3			
I2	I	Close the left foot to first position,		
	2	and lower the heels.		
	3		⎭	

59

13	1	Step forward with the left foot, on the toes.	
	2		
	3		
14	1	Step forward with the right foot, on the toes.	
	2		
	3		
15	1	Step forward with the left foot, on the toes.	Double L.
	2		
	3		
16	1	Close the right foot to first position, lowering	
	2	the heels.	
	3		

B. 2.

1	1	Take a small step back with the right foot.	
	2		
	3		
2	1	Make a little bow to the left side.	
	2		
	3		
3	1	Raise the body again.	Reprise R.
	2		
	3		
4	1	Bring the left foot back to first position.	
	2		
	3	Rise on the toes.	

5	1	Drop on to the outside foot, relaxing the inside knee,	
	2	and make a slight turn away from your partner.	
	3	Rise on the toes and face forward again.	
6	1	Lower both heels together.	
	2		
	3	Rise on the toes.	
7	1	Drop on to the outside foot, relaxing the inside knee,	Branle.
	2	but this time look back at partner over your shoulder.	
	3	Rise on the toes, and face forward again.	
8	1	Lower both heels together.	
	2		
	3		

FIG. V. DANCE FOR THREE

From the Miniature in the Paris Guiglielmo Codex, circa 1463
(Paris : **Bib**. Nat. fonds it., 973)

FIG. VI. DANCE OF THE PERIOD OF DOMENICO DI FERRARA

Detail from the Fresco, " The Wedding of Jacob and Rachel," by Benozzo Gozzoli

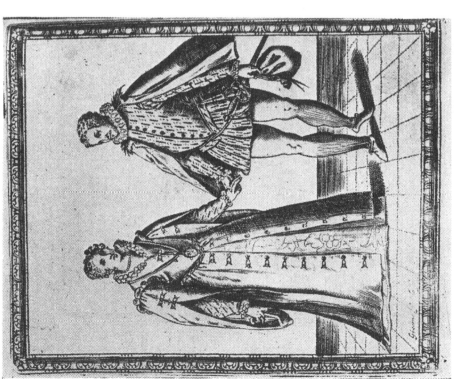

Fig. VII. MANNER OF HOLDING HANDS, 16TH CENTURY, ITALIAN

From " Nobiltà di Dame," by Fabritio Caroso, 1600

Dances

15th Century Italian

BASSE DANCE

STEPS USED IN ITALIAN BASSE DANCE

Both French and Italians used Simples, Doubles and Reprises in their Basse Dances, but they were made in different ways. The Italians set great store by certain graces, which were destined to become the foundation of all dance technique up to the end of the Eighteenth Century. For this reason it is worth while to treat them in detail.

(1) Aiere, or elevation, means rising on the toes, and then lowering the heels smoothly. This rising and falling needs perfect control of the instep ; a control which is only possible when the weight of the body is poised directly over the supporting foot. This, in turn, means that steps must be small.

(2) Maniera, or Manner, is a turning of the body in opposition to the forward foot. (That is to say, in stepping forward with the left foot the turn is to the left ; but it is also made to the left in stepping back with the right foot.) The turn is made before beginning the step, and the shoulder is brought back to its normal position as the heels are lowered at the end.

Aiere and Maniera combined, without making a step, were called " Movimento," and used in some dances as a movement of courtesy. It is helpful to practise Aiere and Maniera in three ways : (1) as Movimento ; (2) combined with a Simple ; and (3) combined with a Double ; because the action is the same but differently timed.

Movimento alone was always made to a count of two :

(1) In rising on the toes make one-eighth of a turn to the left by putting the left shoulder back (but do not drop it).

(2) Bring the shoulder forward to its normal position as the heels are lowered.

The action of raising and lowering the heels, and the action of turning the body, must be smooth and perfectly co-ordinated.

Practise this also, turning to the right.

61

Movimento, being a duple time step, was not used in Basse Dance; it is only given here to help towards the understanding of the steps that follow.

SIMPLE.

The principle is the same when Movimento is combined with a Simple, but in this case it is spread over a count of six. The point to be noted is that we do not count from one to six, but from six to five because rising on the toes and turning the shoulder must be done before the step is made on the first beat of the bar. It is easier to follow the modern practice and think of the six beats as two bars of triple time.

Bar. Beat.

Bar	Beat		
4	1		
	2		
	3	Rise on the toes, making one-eighth turn to the left.	
1	1	Step forward with the left foot, on the toes.	⎫ Begin to bring the
	2		⎬ shoulder forward
	3		⎭ evenly.
2	1	Close the right foot to first position.	
	2	Completing the shoulder movement as the heels are lowered.	
	3		

This leaves a beat free for the rise on the toes and turn to the right for the step with the right foot which usually follows.

Practice Simples with left and right feet alternately.

DOUBLE.

In making a Double, the Movimento must be spread over four bars, making the rise and turn in the fourth bar of the preceding phrase.

Bar. Beat.

Bar	Beat		
4	1		
	2		
	3	Rise on the toes, making one-eighth turn to the left.	
1	1	Step forward with the left foot, on the toes.	⎫
	2		
	3		
2	1	Step forward with the right foot, on the toes.	
	2		⎬ Bringing the
	3		shoulder forward
3	1	Step forward with the left foot, on the toes.	smoothly.
	2		
	3		⎭
4	1	Close right foot to first position, finishing the shoulder movement as	
	2	the heels are lowered.	
	3		

In describing the dance the words "shade the shoulder" and "shoulder level" have been used to indicate the beginning and end of the Movimento.

Notice the difference between the French and Italian styles, the French having a downward and the Italian an upward inflection.

Movimento was also used in the step called "Continenza." The "Continenza" was really a Simple made to the side, and—like a Simple—it occupied two bars of music. Like Simples, Continenze were made in pairs, usually to left and right; they correspond to the two Simples to the side made in the Estampie, and therefore to the French Basse Dance step called "Branle."

Bar.	Beat.	
4	1	
	2	
	3	Rise on the toes, making one-eighth turn to the left.
1	1	Step with the left foot to second position on the toes.
	2	
	3	
2	1	Close right foot to first position, completing the shoulder movement
	2	as the heels are lowered.
	3	

In the Sixteenth Century, Continenze were made with a slight bow; the only information given in Fifteenth-century MSS. is to the effect that Continenze were like Riprese, but should be differentiated by making the Riprese more slowly. In effect, the Italian Reprise was a Simple made sideways but extended to occupy four bars.

RIPRESA. (Reprise.).

Bar.	Beat.	
4	1	
	2	
	3	Rise on the toes, making one-eighth turn to the left.
1	1	Step with the left foot to second position on the toes.
	2	
	3	
2	1	Close the right foot to first position on the toes.
	2	
	3	
3	1	Lower the heels slowly, completing the shoulder movement.
	2	
	3	
4	1	
	2	
	3	

Practise Ripresa to left and right.

TURNING STEPS.

Two kinds of turning step are used in the Basse Dance "Zinevra."

MEZZA VOLTA. (Half turn.).

Bars. Beat.

4   1
    2
    3   Rise on the toes.
1   1   Pivot on the left foot, making a half turn left to face in the opposite
    2   direction, and step with the right foot to second position.
    3
2   1   Close the left to first position, and lower the heels.
    2
    3

VOLTA TONDA. (Whole turn.).

This needs eight bars because it consists of two Simples and a Ripresa.

Bar. Beat.

4   1
    2
    3   Rise on the toes.
1   1   Pivot on the left foot, stepping across with the right to   ⎫
    2   make a quarter turn to the left.   ⎬ Simple
    3   ⎪ turning.
2   1   Close the left foot to first position and lower the heels.   ⎭
    2
    3   Rise on the toes.
3   1   Step on the left foot, to make a quarter turn to the left.   ⎫
    2   ⎬ Simple
    3   ⎪ turning.
4   1   Close the right foot to first position and lower the heels.   ⎭
    2
    3   Rise on the toes.
1   1   Pivot slowly on the left foot, making a half turn to the   ⎫
    2   left.   ⎪
    3   ⎪
2   1   Step with the right foot to second position, on the toes.   ⎬
    2   ⎪ Ripresa
    3   ⎪ turning.
3   1   Close the left foot to first position, on the toes.   ⎪
    2   ⎪
    3   ⎪
4   1   Lower the heels.   ⎪
    2   ⎭
    3

" RIVERENZA."

The Italian " Riverenza " was exactly like the French Révérence in the Fifteenth Century. The lady should make the same movements as the gentleman.

64

Example VIII

Tenor "El Re di Spagna" arranged for the
ITALIAN BASSE DANSE "ZINEVRA"

Arranged by Elsie Palmer

EXAMPLE VIII

"ZINEVRA."

Basse Dance for two composed by Guglielmo Ebreo. This dance begins in file, the lady standing three or four paces behind her partner. There is no preliminary Riverenza; they go straight into the dance. Both use the same steps and the same feet.

Bar. Beat.

Rise on the toes and shade the left shoulder.

Bar.	Beat.		
A. 1	1	Step forward with the left foot, on the toes.	
	2		
	3		Simple, left forward.
2	1	Close right to first position, lower heels,	
	2	bringing the shoulder level.	
	3	Rise on toes, shade the right shoulder.	
3	1	Step forward with the right foot, on the toes.	
	2		
	3		Simple, right forward.
4	1	Close left to first position, lower heels,	
	2	bringing shoulder level.	
	3	Rise on toes, shade left shoulder.	
5	1	Step forward with the left, on the toes.	
	2		
	3		
6	1	Step forward with the right, on the toes.	
	2		
	3		Double, left forward.
7	1	Step forward with the left, on the toes.	
	2		
	3		
8	1	Close right to first position, lower heels,	
	2	bringing shoulder level.	
	3		
9	1	Draw back the right foot, leaving weight	
	2	forward on the left.	
	3		
10	1	Bend the left knee and relax right.	
	2		
	3		Riverenza with the
11	1	Straighten left knee.	right.
	2		
	3		
12	1	Close right to first position.	
	2		
	3	Rise on toes, shade the right shoulder.	

During the next six bars they exchange places, but at the same time they turn about, so in effect their position will be the same, the lady being behind her partner, but facing in the opposite direction to that in which the dance began.

Bar.	Beat.		
A. 13	1	Step forward with the right, on the toes.	Simple, right.
	2		Gentleman only makes
	3		a half turn left.
14	1	Close left to first position, lower heels,	Lady goes forward to
	2	bringing shoulder level.	pass left shoulders.
	3	Rise on toes, shade left shoulder.	
15	1	Step forward with the left, on the toes.	
	2		
	3		Simple, left.
16	1	Close right to first position, lower heels,	
	2	bringing shoulder level.	
	3	Rise on toes, shading right shoulder.	
17	1	Step forward with the right, on the toes.	Simple, right.
	2		Lady only makes a
	3		half turn left to fall
18	1	Close left to first position, lower heels,	in behind her part-
	2	bringing shoulder level.	ner Gentleman
	3	Rise on toes, shade left shoulder.	goes forward.
B. 1	1	Step with the left to second position, on	
	2	the toes.	
	3		
2	1	Close right to first position, on the toes.	
	2		
	3		Ripresa to left.
3	1	Lower heels slowly, bringing shoulder level.	
	2		
	3		
4	1		
	2		
	3	Rise on toes.	
5	1	Step across with the right, on the toes,	
	2	making a quarter turn left.	
	3		Simple, right, making
6	1	Close left to first position, lower heels.	a quarter turn left.
	2		
	3	Rise on toes.	
7	1	Step with left, on the toes, making a quarter	
	2	turn left.	
	3		Simple, left, making
8	1	Close right to first position, lower heels.	a quarter turn left.
	2		
	3	Rise on toes.	

68

Bar. *Beat.*

B. 9 1 Make a half turn on the left foot and step to
       2   second position with the right, on the
       3   toes.
  10 1 Close left to first position, on the toes.
       2
       3   Ripresa, making a half
  11 1 Lower the heels.   turn to the left.
       2
       3
  12 1
       2
       3 Rise on the toes and shade left shoulder.

  13 1 Small step to second position with the left.
       2
       3   Continenza to the left.
  14 1 Close right to first position, lowering the
       2   heels.
       3

  15 1 Small step to second position with the right.
       2
       3   Continenza to the
  16 1 Close left to first position, lowering the   right.
       2   heels.
       3 Rise on the toes.

Repeat A. and B.

The dancers are now facing in the opposite direction to that in which the dance began. The Lady stands behind her partner as before. In this position they begin again at the beginning, and repeat all the steps given above. At the end of the repeat they will be standing as they were at the beginning of the dance facing forward. In beginning the next step, the gentleman must make a half-turn to take the lady's right hand. They take hands in a manner peculiar to this school of dancing, linking their little fingers with the hands raised to shoulder level, but the elbows should not be raised. The first three fingers should be closed over the thumb.

Bar. *Beat.*

C. 1 1 Step forward with the left, on the toes.
       2
       3   Simple with left.
   2 1 Close the right to first position, and lower
       2   the heels.
       3 Rise on the toes.

69

C. 3   1   Step forward with the right, on the toes.
       2
       3
   4   1   Close the left to first position, and lower   } Simple with right.
       2   the heels.
       3   Rise on the toes.

   5   1   Step forward with the left, on the toes.
       2
       3
   6   1   Step forward with the right, on the toes.   } Double with the left.
       2
       3   With these two Sim-
   7   1   Step forward with the left, on the toes.   ples and a Double
       2   they   exchange
       3   places.
   8   1   Close the right to first position, and lower
       2   the heels.
       3   Rise on the toes.

Repeat C.

On the end of the last step they release hands in order to make a half turn and take left hands in the same way. The last eight bars are repeated, but beginning with the right foot instead of the left. At the end of this movement they should be in their original positions, but the gentleman faces his partner. They have released hands.

B. Second Time.

Bar. Beat.

   1   1   Take the left foot back to fourth position.
       2
       3
   2   1   Bend the right knee, keeping the weight
       2   forward over it. Relax the left.
       3   Riverenza with the
   3   1   Straighten the right knee.   } left.
       2
       3
   4   1   Close the left to first position.
       2
       3   Rise on the toes.

Bar. Beat.

5	1 2	Step forward with the left on the toes, making a quarter turn left.	Simple with the left. On this step they make each quarter turn left, to finish back to back.
6	3 1 2 3	Close the right to first position, and lower the heels. Rise on the toes.	

7	1 2	Step with the right to small second position, making a half turn to the left.	Simple with the right, making a half turn left, to face partner.
8	3 1 2 3	Close the left foot to first position, and lower the heels. Rise on the toes.	

9	1 2	Step across with the right to second position, making a quarter turn left.	Simple with the right, making a quarter turn left.
10	3 1 2 3	Close left foot to first position, and lower the heels. Rise on the toes.	

11	1 2	Step with left, on the toes, making a quarter turn left.	Simple with the left, making a quarter turn left.
12	3 1 2 3	Close right to first position, lower heels. Rise on the toes.	

13	1 2 3	Make a half turn on the left and step to second position with the right, on the toes.	
14	1 2 3	Close left to first position, on the toes.	Ripresa right, making a half turn to the left.
15	1 2 3	Lower the heels, slowly.	
16	1 2 3	Rise on the toes, shade left shoulder.	

A. 2.

Bar. Beat.

1	1	Step forward with the left, on the toes.
	2	
	3	
2	1	Step forward with the right, on the toes.
	2	
	3	
3	1	Step forward with the left, on the toes.
	2	
	3	
4	1	Close right to first position, lower heels,
	2	bringing shoulder level.
	3	Rise on the toes, shade right shoulder.

Double forward with the left. Pass right shoulders.

5	1	Step forward with the right, on the toes.
	2	
	3	
6	1	Step forward with the left, on the toes.
	2	
	3	
7	1	Step forward with the right, on the toes.
	2	
	3	
8	1	Close the left to first position, lower the
	2	heels, bringing shoulder level.
	3	Rise on the toes.

Double forward with the right, curving in slightly to the right.

9	1	Make a half turn on the right foot, and step
	2	to second position with the left, on the
	3	toes.
10	1	Close right to first position, on the toes.
	2	
	3	
11	1	Lower the heels slowly.
	2	
	3	
12	1	
	2	
	3	Rise on the toes, shade the right shoulder.

Ripresa with the left, making a half turn to the right.

A. 2.

Bar. Beat.

13	1	Step with the right to second position, on	
	2	the toes. (No turn.)	
	3		
14	1	Close the left to first position, on the toes.	
	2		Ripresa to the right, without making a turn.
	3		
15	1	Lower the heels slowly, bringing shoulder	
	2	level.	
	3		
16	1		
	2		
	3		

17	1	Take the left foot back to fourth position.	
	2		
	3		
18	1	Bend the right knee, keeping the weight	
	2	forward over it. Relax the left.	
	3		Riverenza with the left foot.
19	1	Straighten the right knee.	
	2		
	3		
20	1	Close the left to first position.	
	2		
	3	Rise on the toes, shade the left shoulder.	

B. THIRD TIME.

Bar. Beat.

1	1	Step forward with the left, on the toes.	
	2		
	3		Simple forward with the left.
2	1	Close the right to first position, lower heels,	
	2	bringing shoulders level.	
	3		

3	1	Step forward with the right, on the toes.	
	2		
	3		Simple forward with the right.
4	1	Close the left to first position, lower the	
	2	heels, bringing shoulder level.	
	3	Rise on the toes, shade the left shoulder.	

73

B. THIRD TIME.

Bar. Beat.

5   1 Step forward with the left, on the toes.
     2
     3
6   1 Step forward with the right, on the toes.
     2
     3
7   1 Step forward with the left, on the toes.
     2
     3
8   1 Close the right to first position, lower the
     2   heels, bringing the shoulder level.
     3 Rise on the toes.

> Double forward with the left to meet partner.

9   1 Step across with the right, on the toes,
     2   making a quarter turn to the left.
     3
10 1 Close the left to first position, lower the
     2   heels.
     3 Rise on the toes.

> Simple with the right, making a quarter turn left.

11 1 Step with the left, on the toes, making a
     2   quarter turn to the left.
     3
12 1 Close the right to first position, lower the
     2   heels.
     3 Rise on the toes.

> Simple with the left, making a quarter turn left.

13 1 Make a half turn on the left foot, and step
     2   to second position with the right, on the
     3   toes.
14 1 Close the left to first position, on the toes.
     2
     3
15 1 Lower the heels slowly.
     2
     3
16 1
     2
     3

> Ripresa, making a half turn left.

B. Fourth Time.

Bar. *Beat.*

1	1	Take the left foot back to fourth position.	
	2		
	3		
2	1	Bend the right knee, keeping the weight	
	2	forward over it. Relax the left.	Riverenza with the
	3		left foot, they touch
3	1	Straighten the right knee.	right hands lightly.
	2		
	3		
4	1	Close the left to first position.	
	2		
	3	Rise on the toes, shade the left shoulder.	

In rising from this Riverenza the lady must make a quarter turn right, to face front, placing herself beside her partner. They take inside hands by linking their little fingers and raising the hands to shoulder level.

Bar. *Beat.*

5	1	Step with the left to second position, on the	
	2	toes. (No turn.)	
	3		
6	1	Close the right to first position, on the toes.	
	2		
	3		
7	1	Lower the heels slowly, bringing the shoulder	Ripresa to the left.
	2	level.	
	3		
8	1		
	2		
	3	Rise on the toes, shade the right shoulder.	
9	1	Step with the right to second position on	
	2	toes. (No turn.)	
	3		
10	1	Close the left to first position, on the toes.	
	2		
	3		
11	1	Lower the heels slowly, bringing the shoulder	Ripresa to the right.
	2	level.	
	3		
12	1	They release hands.	
	2		
	3		

75

B. FOURTH TIME.

Bar. *Beat.*

13	1	Take the left foot back to fourth position.	
	2		
	3		
14	1	Bend the right knee, keeping the weight	
	2	forward over it. Relax the left.	
	3		Riverenza with the
15	1	Straighten the right knee.	left foot.
	2		
	3		
16	1	Close the left to first position.	
	2		
	3		

Example IX

Ballo composed by Domenico di Ferrara
PREXONERA
Arranged by Elsie Palmer

Dances

15th Century Italian

BALLI

STEPS AS THEY ARE COUNTED IN PREXONERA

BOW AND CURTSEY. (Riverenza.)

Bar. Beat.

I   I ⎫

2 ⎪ Take the left foot back, bend right knee and relax the left, keeping

3 ⎬   the weight forward and the head up.

4 ⎪

5 ⎭ Rise, bringing the left foot to first position again.

6

TWO CONTINENZE.

Bar. Beat.

    6 ⎫ Shade the left shoulder, rising on the toes.

I   I ⎬ Small step to the left, on the toes.

    2 ⎭ Close right to first, bring shoulder forward, lower heels.

    3 ⎫ Shade the left shoulder, rising on the toes.

    4 ⎬ Small step to the left, on the toes.

    5 ⎭ Close right to first, bring shoulder forward, lower heels.

    6

TWO SIMPLES.

Bar. Beat.

    6 ⎫ Shade the left shoulder, rising on the toes.

I   I ⎬ Step forward left, on the toes.

    2 ⎭ Close right to first, bring shoulder forward, lower heels.

    3 ⎫ Shade the right shoulder, rising on the toes.

    4 ⎬ Step forward right, on the toes.

    5 ⎭ Close left to first, bring shoulder forward, lower heels.

    6

One Double.

Bar. *Beat.*

6\ Shade the left shoulder, rising on the toes.

1   1 | Step forward left, on the toes.

    2 | Step forward right, on the toes.   Bring shoulder for-

    3 | Step forward left, on the toes.   ward gradually.

    4 | Close right to first, lower heels.

    5/ Pause.

    6

Saltarello Double.

Bar. *Beat.*

6 \ Shade the left shoulder, rising on the toes.

1   1 | Step forward left, on the toes.

    2

    3 | Step forward right, on the toes.

    4 | Step forward left, on the toes.

    5/ Hop left, bringing right forward. Lower left heel after hop.

    6

Piva Double. (4/4 time.)

Bar. *Beat.*

1   1 \ Step forward left.

    2 } Step forward right, on the toes.

    3/ Step forward left. (Not on the toes.)

    4

Movimento.

Bar. *Beat.*

1   1 Shade left shoulder.   } Rising on the toes.

    2 Bring shoulder level.   J

    3 Lower heels.

    4

EXAMPLE IX

PREXONERA (BALLO)

Composed by Domenico of Ferrara

This is a dance for two. They stand side by side, the lady on her partner's right. When it is time for them to take hands, they do so by linking their little fingers and bending the forearm back to shoulder level.

79

Begin with the music called "Intrata.".

Bar. Beat.

E. 1   1
       2
       3   The gentleman takes off his hat.
       4
       5
       6

   2   1
       2   Take the left foot back.
       3
       4
       5   Bend right knee for the bow, relaxing the left.
       6

   3   1
       2   Straighten the knees.
       3
       4
       5   Close the left foot.
       6

   4   1
       2
       3   The gentleman puts on his hat.
       4
       5
       6

   5   1
       2   They take hands as described above.
       3

In this period it was not usual to give exact movements for bows and curtsies. The timing given above is only a suggestion to help beginners. The third beat in bar 5 will be the preparation for the first step in the dance.

A. 1.

Bar. Beat.

       3 ⎫
   1   1 ⎬ Continenza to the left.
       2 ⎭

       3 ⎫
       4 ⎬ Continenza to the left.
       5 ⎭

       6 ⎫
   2   1 ⎬ Simple forward with the left.
       2 ⎭

       3 ⎫
       4 ⎬ Simple forward with the right.
       5 ⎭

80

A. I.

Bar.	Beat.	
2	6	} Simple forward with the left.
3	I	
	2	
	3	} Double forward with the right.
	4	
	5	
	6	
4	I	
	2	
	3	} Riverenza with the left.
	4	
	5	
	6	
5	I	
	2	
	3	

A. 2.

The whole section is repeated, and at the end of the repeat they release hands. The lady stands still, and the gentleman goes forward alone.

B. I.

Bar.	Beat.	
I	3	} Simple forward with the left.
	I	
	2	
	3	} Simple forward with the right.
	4	
	5	
	6	
2	I	
	2	} Double forward with the left.
	3	
	4	
	5	
	6	
3	I	
	2	} Double forward with the right.
	3	
	4	
	5	
	6	

Now the gentleman stands still, and in bars 4, 5, and 6, the lady follows him. She makes the two Simples and two Doubles as he did, and stands behind him.

But in bar 6 the gentleman must turn round in his place so that he faces the lady, and they take right hands to make two Simples, changing places, and a Riverenza.

B. 1.

Bar. Beat.

7	6 1 2	Simple with the left.
	3 4 5	Simple with the right.
8	6 1 2 3 4 5 6	Riverenza with the left.

B. 2.

Repeat from B. 1, but this time the lady goes forward first, and the gentleman follows ; the lady makes the turn to face her partner in the 6th bar. In bars 7 and 8 they go round as before, but this time they must finish side by side, facing forward, and take inside hands as at the beginning of the dance. They go forward side by side.

The music changes to 4/4.

Bar. Beat.

C. 1	1 2 3 4	Piva Double with the left.
2	1 2 3 4	Piva Double with the right.
3	1 2 3 4	Piva Double with the left.
4	1 2 3 4	Piva Double with the right.

Repeat these four bars, using the same steps. Then they stop.

Bar. *Beat.*

C. 5   1
     2 } Movimento, gentleman alone.
     3
     4

6   1
    2 } Movimento, lady alone.
    3
    4

7   1
    2 } Together, they make four very small steps away from each other.
    3
    4

8   1
    2 } Movimento, lady alone.
    3
    4

9   1
    2 } Movimento, gentleman alone.
    3
    4

10   1
     2 } Four very small steps away, as before.
     3
     4

11   1
     2 } Movimento made by both at the same time.
     3
     4

The music changes to 6/4.

D. 1   4
    1
    2 } Saltarello Double to meet, face forward, and take hands.
    3
    4
    5

Bar.	Beat.	
D. 2	6 1 2 3 4 5	} Saltarello Double forward, with right.
3	6 1 2 3 4 5	} Saltarello Double forward, with left.
4	6 1 2 3 4 5 6	} Saltarello Double forward with right.

The five bars of the Intrata may be used to walk back to where the dance began, because the dance is repeated from the beginning, but in the repeat the lady goes first every time and the gentleman does whatever the lady did the first time.

THE STEPS AS THEY ARE COUNTED IN ANELLO

RIVERENZA.

Bar.	Beat.	
1	1	Take the left foot back.
	2	
	3	Bend right knee and relax the left, keeping the weight forward, and head up.
	4	
2	1	Straighten the knees.
	2	
	3	Bring the left foot to first position again.
	4	

SALTARELLO DOUBLE.

Bar. *Beat.*

	4	Shade the left shoulder.	
1	1	Step forward left, on the toes.	⎫
	2		⎪
	3	Step forward right, on the toes.	⎬ Gradually bring shoulder forward.
	4		⎪
2	1	Step forward left, on the toes.	⎭
	2		
	3	Small hop on left, bring right forward.	
	4	Shade right shoulder.	

You are now ready to repeat the Double, beginning with the right foot.

MOVIMENTO.

Bar. *Beat.*

1	1	Shade the left shoulder.	⎫ Rising on the toes.
	2	Bring left shoulder level.	⎭
	3	Lower the heels.	
	4		

VOLTA TONDA. (Whole turn in place.)

In this dance the Volta Tonda is a plain Double turning in place, like the "Turn Single" in English Country Dancing.

Bar. *Beat.*

1	1	Step left, quarter turn to left.
	2	
	3	Step right, quarter turn to left.
	4	
2	1	Step left, quarter turn to left.
	2	
	3	Close right, quarter turn to left.
	4	

PIVA DOUBLE.

Bar. *Beat.*

1	1	Step forward left.
	2	Step forward right, on the toes.
	3	Step forward left.
	4	

RIPRESA.

Bar. Beat.

1   1 Rise on the toes and step with the right to second position.

     2

     3 Close the left to first position, on the toes.

     4

2   1 Lower the heels.

     2

     3

     4

EXAMPLE X

ANELLO : BALLO FOR FOUR

COMPOSED BY DOMENICO OF FERRARA

The second couple stands four paces behind the first couple, the ladies on the right of their partners. Partners hold hands by linking little fingers as described in the instructions for Prexonera.

A. 1.

Bar. Beat.

1   1

     2

     3

     4   } Saltarello Double with the left. Forward.

2   1

     2

     3

     4

3   1

     2

     3

     4   } Saltarello Double with the right. Forward.

4   1

     2

     3

     4

A. 2.

Bar. *Beat.*

Bar	Beat	
1	1	
	2	
	3	
	4	Saltarello Double with the left. Forward.
2	1	
	2	
	3	
	4	

Bar	Beat	
3	1	
	2	
	3	
	4	Saltarello Double with the right. Forward.
4	1	
	2	
	3	
	4	

A. 3.

Bar. *Beat.*

Bar	Beat	
1	1	
	2	
	3	
	4	Saltarello Double with the left. Forward.
2	1	
	2	
	3	
	4	

Bar	Beat	
3	1	
	2	
	3	
	4	Saltarello Double with the right. Forward.
4	1	
	2	
	3	
	4	

At this point they release hands, and during the last two Saltarello Doubles they open out into a square, the front couple making a turn to the left in order to face the second couple.

A. 4.

Bar.	Beat.	
5	1	
	2	
	3	
	4	Saltarello Double with left.
6	1	
	2	
	3	
	4	
7	1	
	2	
	3	
	4	Saltarello Double with right.
8	1	
	2	
	3	
	4	

B. 1.

Bar.	Beat.	
1	1	
	2	
	3	Movimento. Gentlemen only.
	4	
2	1	
	2	
	3	Movimento. Ladies only.
	4	
3	1	
	2	
	3	
	4	Saltarello Double with left.
4	1	
	2	
	3	
	4	
5	1	
	2	
	3	
	4	
6	1	Saltarello Double with right.
	2	
	3	
	4	

With these two Doubles, the gentlemen exchange places, passing right shoulders, and finishing with a half-turn to face each other again.

88

B. 2.

Repeat B. But this time the ladies make the Movimento first, and exchange places.

C. 1.

Bar. Beat.

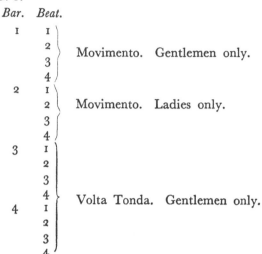

1	1	
	2	} Movimento. Gentlemen only.
	3	
	4	
2	1	
	2	} Movimento. Ladies only.
	3	
	4	
3	1	
	2	
	3	
	4	} Volta Tonda. Gentlemen only.
4	1	
	2	
	3	
	4	

C. 2.

These four bars are repeated ; but the ladies make the Movimento first, and the Volta Tonda.

D. 1.

Bar. Beat.

1	1	
	2	} Piva Double.
	3	
	4	
2	1	
	2	} Piva Double.
	3	
	4	
3	1	
	2	} Piva Double.
	3	
	4	
4	1	
	2	} Piva Double.
	3	
	4	

With these four Piva Doubles the gentlemen cross over, pass behind the contrary lady, and regain their original places.

89

D. 2.

These four bars are repeated, and the ladies do as the gentlemen did, but they will pass behind their partners, because the gentlemen have changed places.

D. 3.

Bar.	Beat.	
1	1 2 3 4	Movimento made by gentlemen to the contrary ladies.
2	1 2 3 4	Movimento made by ladies to the contrary gentlemen.
3	1 2 3 4	Movimento made by gentlemen to their partners.
4	1 2	Movimento made by ladies to their partners.
	3 4	The first couple must make a half turn to face forward.
E. 1	1 2 3	Gentlemen make a Ripresa with the right, to step near to their
2	1 2 3	partners.
3	1 2 3	All take hands as at the beginning of the dance.
4	1 2 3	

The whole dance is repeated, but this time the ladies do everything first.

Example X — Ballo composed by Domenico di Ferrara

ANELLO

Arranged by Elsie Palmer

Historical Notes

16th Century

SIXTEENTH CENTURY

The Sixteenth Century may be regarded as the end of the old world or the beginning of the new, according to the point of view. In dancing, as in costume and other things affecting social life, there was a clean break during the first quarter of the Seventeenth Century, with a fresh start on new lines. In the Sixteenth Century, the forms dating from the Twelfth Century were gathered up and worked out to their logical conclusion.

A large volume would be needed to contain the history of dancing in the Sixteenth Century. Not only national, but also regional characteristics emerged, and there was more distinction between the court and country dances (nevertheless, there is ample evidence to show that courtiers enjoyed dancing with the country folk ; and enough to suggest that country folk attempted the courtly style).

Since it is impossible to do justice to the whole of Europe in a small space, it seems best to concentrate on England ; firstly because the Sixteenth Century was a golden age in which we earned the title of " the dancing English " ; secondly, because we want to relate dancing to our own history, and in so doing to consider the influences which reached us from abroad.

In 1501 Katherine of Aragon came to England to marry Henry VII's elder son, Prince Arthur. Both music and dancing played a large part in Spanish court life, and it is more than probable that Katherine brought the Pavane to this country. Arbeau (Orchésographie) gives two distinct types of Pavane—one Spanish and the other presumably French. Since Sixteenth-century writers usually refer to the Pavane as a Spanish dance, we must suppose the Spanish to be the original form ; certainly it would be the one known to Katherine of Aragon.

The Spanish Pavane, given by Arbeau, belongs to the Tordion family,[1] though he obscures the fact by writing the air in duple time. Early Spanish music written for the Pavane is in triple time and Galliard rhythm, though not in strict Galliard phrasing. The fact that the Spanish Pavane was practically a Galliard is confirmed by the Bodleian MS. Douce 280, where it is described as being " formed with bounds and capers " ; the springing passages are set between sections made up of a few slow steps.

Many Sixteenth-century steps are used in Spanish dancing to-day, and anyone who has seen a fine Spanish dancer perform the Aragonese Jota will know how gaiety can be combined with tremendous dignity and restraint. The Spanish

---

[1] Example XII (*a*), p.100.

Pavane should be interpreted in this way ; it is a style which presents great difficulties to us because it is contrary to our national temperament. There is no reason to suppose that this was any less true in the reign of Henry VIII, and it may account in part for the fact that all the well-known English Pavane music was written in the French idiom.

In France, as in England, Pavane and Galliard were not originally linked together. Thus, Arena, writing in the first quarter of the century, tells us that Pavanes were not much danced ; later on he tells his friends of a new and graceful Galliard coming into fashion which will make their bodies sweat exceedingly. This suggests a more boisterous style than that of Spain.

The pedigree of French Galliard[1] is easily established ; it was derived from the old Branle Gai through the Estampie Gai, the Pas de Brébant and the Tordion. Four springs and a cadence formed the Tordion step, and for the Galliard the four springs were elaborated in various ways. Four springs and a cadence were called a Passage ; a Passage begun with the left foot must be repeated, beginning with the right foot. The emphasis was on energy and agility rather than subtlety and restraint, and following these lines the Galliard eventually ceased to be a dance and became an acrobatic display. This was especially true in England, where Galliard dancing was treated as a sport ; it was undertaken for exercise. In " The Castel of Helth " Sir Thomas Elyot classed it as " very vehement exercise " ; and, under the eagle eye of Queen Elizabeth, Englishmen spun round longer, and leaped higher, than the men of other nations. In this connection it should be remembered that whilst Mediæval gentlemen could fight in tournaments to show off before their ladies, Sixteenth-century gentlemen were largely deprived of this outlet. Sport, as we understand it, had not been invented ; so the Elizabethan gentlemen danced Galliards.

To return to King Henry VIII ; if Spanish fashions were favoured at the beginning of his reign, they were soon displaced by new ideas from France. The tide was turning in 1514, when Henry's sister Mary went to France to marry Louis XII, taking with her a lady-in-waiting called Anne Boleyn. The following year King Louis died and was succeeded by Francis I, a young man of glamorous personality and soaring ambitions equal to those of Henry himself. Mary returned to England, and so did Anne Boleyn. In 1521 Robert Coplande published instructions for dancing Basse Dances " after the manner of France " ; they were attached to a French Grammar intended for the use of young gentlemen attending the Field of the Cloth of Gold.

According to Sir Thomas Elyot (The Boke named the Governour) the dances used in England in 1531 were Basse Dances, Bargenettes, Pavions, Turgions, and Rounds ; he does not mention the Galliard until 1534 (The Castel of Helth), so its introduction to this country must have been between those dates. By 1534 Henry had married Anne Boleyn, and French fashions were the order of the day.

The two English collections of Basse Dances contain several examples in common with the Burgundian MS. and Toulouze, but also a number of dances not found elsewhere.

[1] Examples XIII and XIII (a).

Musical evidence shows the Bargenettes (Bergerettes) to have been Caroles in Branle form.

At this early date the Pavion is most likely to have been the Spanish Pavane. The Turgion was the Tordion, here separated from the Basse Dance.

The Rounds would be the English Rounds, as distinguished from the French Brawls. The English Round was never a Branle, because it was not a linked dance, and it lacked the characteristic sway from left to right.

One thing is absent from this picture of early Tudor dancing. Apart from a dance called " la Basse Danse de Venise " in the Salisbury collection there is no evidence of Italian influence in England ; yet many years later Queen Elizabeth was to tell the French Ambassador that in her youth she had danced high in the Italian manner.

The disturbed reigns of Edward VI and Mary were not favourable to the development of social graces ; but the accession of Queen Elizabeth produced the exact conditions in which dancing does develop. A good performer herself, Elizabeth demanded the highest standards from her Court. The luckless Maid of Honour who did not dance well enough to satisfy her royal mistress was liable to be reprimanded before the whole assembly.

It has been said that Queen Elizabeth chose Sir Christopher Hatton for high office on account of his Galliard dancing. Now the Queen could appreciate an elegant man as well as any other woman, but enough has been said already to show that an outstanding Galliard dancer was no carpet knight ; he must possess a fund of energy, coupled with patience and application to carry him through many hours of practice ; a clear brain, and quick decision.

Queen Elizabeth encouraged Galliard dancing at Court. One Pavane[1] was danced at the beginning of the ball for the benefit of " the most eminent who were no longer very young " (von Wedel, 1585, in " Queen Elizabeth and Some Foreigners " ; ed. Victor von Kearwill), after which the young people danced Galliards.

Shakespeare mentions " La Volta " and the " Coranto " (" Henry V," Act III, Scene 5) :

> " They bid us to their English dancing-schools,
> And teach lavoltas high and swift corantos ;
> Saying our grace is only in our heels,
> And that we are most lofty runaways."

Arbeau's instructions for " La Volta " agree in every particular with the pictures of the dance, especially the way in which the lady keeps one hand on her skirt to prevent it from flying when she makes her leap. The idea of tossing partners in the air comes from folk dance ; it occurs also in Arbeau's " Branle de l'Official," though here the hold is different. " La Volta " should only be danced where the man's part is danced by a man ; it is not suitable for children, or if the man's part is taken by a girl. Nevertheless in this connection it is only fair to say that the Bodleian MS. Douce 280 gives a Spanioletta in which not only does the gentleman " heave up " his partner in his arms, but she proceeds to do as much for him.

[1] Example XII. (b), p. 104

94

The " Coranto " must have been very popular, if we may judge from the amount of music written for it.   The dance might be described as a Farandole danced with Branle steps ; that is to say the steps given by Arbeau move alternately to left and right as in a Branle, but the dancers form a linked line which is led hither and thither at the leader's discretion according to Sir John Davies in his " Poem of Orchestra " :

> " What shall I call those current traverses,
> That on a triple dactyl foot do run
> Close by the ground with sliding passages ?
> Wherein that dancer greatest praise hath won
> Which with best order can all order shun ;
> For everywhere he wantonly must range
> And turn and wind with unexpected change."
>
> (*Stanza* 69.)

There was, however, a tendency towards figure dancing at the end of the Sixteenth Century, and the English " Temple Coranto " shows a rudimentary figure.

The Measures and the Country Dance were regarded as characteristically English.   Now although Shakespeare makes Beatrice describe the Measures as being " full of state and ancientry " (" Much Ado About Nothing," Act II, Scene 1) there is no mention of the dance before the late Sixteenth Century. Sir John Davies describes the bewildering variety of the Measures in his poem of " Orchestra " ; " yet," he concludes :

> " All the feet whereon these Measures goe
> Are only Spondees, solemne, grave, and slow."

In other words, the Measures were always danced to Pavane music.   There are very few recorded dances called Measures, but without exception they involve dancing *contra tempo*—that is, without regard to the four-bar phrasing of the music. In " The Measure of Heaven and Earth " Galliard passages are danced in Pavane time.   This explains Morley's statement in writing of the Pavane to the effect that " the art of dancing has come to such perfection . . . that any reasonable dancer will make measure of no measure, so that it is no great matter of what number you make your straine."—(Thomas Morley, " Plain and Easy Introduction to Practical Music, Part III, p. 180.)

The Measures were much used in the Court Masques of the next reign.   It is quite clear that Measures in a Masque were elaborate figure dances ; but figure dances may be danced in any rhythm, and it was the fact of dancing cross-rhythms that made the Measure ; not the figure.

Queen Elizabeth prided herself on being, to use her own words, " mere English," and as she grew older she became interested in purely English dances. On her many progresses through the country it had been usual to bring the country people to dance before the Queen.   At Cowdray in 1591 Elizabeth watched Lord and Lady Montague dancing with their tenants, and from this time on there are references to Country dancing at Court.   What were the English country dances

95

at this time ? Nashe gives the names of some of them in " Have with you to Saffron Walden "—" Rogero," " Basilena," " Turkeyloney," " All Flowers of the Broom," " Pepper is Black," " Greensleeves," and " Peggy Ramsey." Four of these dances can be found in " The English Dancing Master " : " Roger " (Ed. 1695), " Broom " (Ed. 1651), " Pepper's Black " (Ed. 1651), and " Greensleeves " (Ed. 1686) ; but it is possible the dance may have altered in the case of the two of late date. " Turkeyloney " and " Basilena " occur in the cycle of Elizabethan MSS. already quoted.

Some changes must have been made in the Country dance after it came to Court, because in 1600 the Maids of Honour were dancing " the old and new country dances."

The English Country Dance will be treated in detail under the Seventeenth Century.

There remain the Almains. It is not clear whether the Almain was preserved by the country folk as the Estampie was. There is a picture of King Henry VIII dancing an Almain,[1] and in it all the dancers wear peasant costume. The presence of a number of Almains in the same MSS. as the country dances " Turkeyloney " and " Basilena " suggests this possibility. They fall into two classes : The Old Almain, and others like it, have music in even sixteen-bar phrases ; the New Almain and its relatives need music in alternating sixteen and twelve-bar phrases. These dances are of particular interest because they show the kind of change that was taking place at the end of the Sixteenth Century.

Dancing in Elizabethan England was not confined to the Court and the village green : in Shakespeare's " Henry V " (Act III, Scene 5) we find one of the French courtiers saying :

> " They bid us to the English dancing-schools,
> And teach lavoltas high and swift corantos."

This must have been pleasantly topical when it was written, because we were, in fact, out-dancing the French at all points. The English dancing schools were one of the sights of London, a source of wonder and interest to all foreign visitors. Two or three times a week there were well-conducted assemblies frequented by the wives and daughters of worthy citizens : when no assembly was in progress there was always the chance of seeing some young man practising Galliard Passages—spinning, leaping and somersaulting.

We were called " the dancing English," and the title seems to have been won by genuine hard work ; not gaiety and assurance alone.

[1] See Figure 1. (Frontispiece).

Dances

16th Century

STEPS USED IN THE SCOTS BRANLE

Most of the steps used in the Scots Branles were Doubles and Simples, but they were made in a particular way. Instead of the pause at the fourth bar there was a hop on the supporting foot and the other was crossed in front. When you are told to " cross " the foot, remember that it should be done as in the Highland Fling, keeping the knee well turned out and bringing the heel just below the other knee, with the toes turned down. There does not seem to have been a special name for this step in the Sixteenth Century; but we can call it a Scots Double for convenience.

Bar.	Beat.		
I	I	Spring on to the left foot in second position.	
	2		
	3	Spring on to the right foot in first position.	Scots Double to the left.
	4		
2	I	Spring on to the left in second position.	
	2		
	3	Hop on left, crossing right.	
	4		

The Simples were made on the same principle.

Bar.	Beat.		
I	I	Spring on to the left foot in second position.	Scots Simple to the left.
	2		
	3	Hop on left, crossing right.	
	4		

A variation is introduced at the end of the second Scots Branle, when the three springs are made in place and the third becomes a Cadence.

Bar.	Beat.	
I	I	Spring on to left, raising the right forward.
	2	
	3	Spring on to right, raising the left forward.
	4	
2	I	Spring on to left, raising the right forward.
	2	
	3	Spring on to right, drawing it back.
	4	Point the left in front with the toe just resting on the ground.

97

In raising the foot forward, the gentlemen might give a good strong kick ;
but the ladies should only lift their foot a few inches from the ground.

The Scots Branle was popular in France at the time of Mary Stuart's marriage
to the Dauphin.

EXAMPLE XI

THE FIRST SCOTS BRANLE. From Arbeau's "Orchésographie."
This is a true Branle, with the dancers holding hands in a ring.

Bar.	Beat.	
1	1	
	2	
	3	
	4	Scots Double to the left.
2	1	
	2	
	3	
	4	
3	1	
	2	
	3	
	4	
4	1	Scots Double to the right.
	2	
	3	
	4	
5	1	
	2	
	3	Scots Simple to the left.
	4	
6	1	
	2	
	3	Scots Simple to the right.
	4	
7	1	
	2	
	3	
	4	Scots Double to the left.
8	1	
	2	
	3	
	4	

Bar.	Beat.	
9	1	
	2	
	3	
	4	Scots Double to the right.
10	1	
	2	
	3	
	4	
11	1	
	2	
	3	Scots Simple to the left.
	4	
12	1	
	2	Scots Simple to the right.
	3	
	4	

THE SECOND SCOTS BRANLE.

Bar.	Beat.	
1	1	
	2	
	3	
	4	Scots Double to the left.
2	1	
	2	
	3	
	4	
3	1	
	2	Scots Simple to the right.
	3	
	4	
4	1	
	2	Scots Simple to the left.
	3	
	4	
5	1	
	2	
	3	
	4	Scots Double to the right.
6	1	
	2	
	3	
	4	

99

THE SECOND SCOTS BRANLE—(continued).

Bar. Beat.

7	1	
	2	
	3	
	4	Scots Double to the left.
8	1	
	2	
	3	
	4	
9	1	
	2	Scots Simple to the right.
	3	
	4	
10	1	Spring on to left, raising the right forward.
	2	
	3	Spring on to right, raising the left forward.
	4	
11	1	Spring on to left, raising the right forward.
	2	
	3	Spring on to the right, drawing it back.
	4	Point the left in front, just touching the ground.

The dancers might dance the first Branle several times before starting the second, or they might dance them alternately.

EXAMPLE XII (A)

THE SPANISH PAVANE. (Arbeau, " Orchésographie." 1588.).

Partners stand side by side, the lady on the right, holding hands without raising them. Bow and curtsy without music (see p. 99).

Bar. Beat.

1	1	Step forward with the left foot, on the toes.	
	2		
	3	Close right to first position, and lower heels.	Simple.
	4		
2	1	Step forward with the right foot, on the toes.	
	2		
	3	Close left to first position, and lower heels.	Simple.
	4		
3	1	Step forward with the left foot, on the toes.	
	2		
	3	Bring the right foot under the left heel, raising left forward.	
	4		

Example XI

MUSIC FOR THE SCOTS' BRANLE

From Arbeau's "Orchésographie"   **First Scots' Branle**

Arranged by Elsie Palmer

Second Scots' Branle

Example XII(a)

SPANISH PAVANE

From Arbeau's "Orchésographie"

Arranged by Elsie Palmer

THE SPANISH PAVANE—(continued).

Bar. Beat.

4	1	Spring on to left foot, raising right forward.	
" and "		Spring on to right foot, raising left forward.	Fleuret L.
	2	Spring on to left foot, raising right forward.	
" and "		Pause.	
	3	Spring on to right foot, raising left forward.	
" and "		Spring on to left foot, raising right forward.	Fleuret R.
	4	Spring on to right foot, raising left forward.	
" and "		Pause.	

5   1 } Fleuret L.
     2

     3 } Fleuret R.
     4

6   1 } Fleuret L.
     2

     3 } Fleuret R.
     4

7   1 } Fleuret L.
     2

     3 } Close right foot to first position.
     4

8   1 Hop on left foot, raising right forward.
     2 Spring on to right, drawing it back to first position, raising the left forward.
     3 Spring on to left, drawing it back to first position, raising the right forward.
     4 Close the right to first position.

The slow steps in bars 1, 2, 3, and 8 remain constant; but more elaborate steps were substituted for the Fleurets when the dance was repeated.

NOTE,—Arbeau writes his Spanish Pavane in duple time, but it should be in triple time and Galliard rhythm.

STEPS USED IN THE PAVANE

DOUBLE.

Bar. Beat.

1	1	Step forward on the toes with the left foot.
	2	
2	1	Step forward with the right, on the toes.
	2	
3	1	Step forward on the toes with the left foot.
	2	
4	1	Close the right to first position, and lower the heels.
	2	

SIMPLE.

Bar. Beat.

1   1 Step forward on the toes with the left foot.
     2

2   1 Close the right to first position, and lower the heels.
     2

REPRISE.

You can use the old Reprise made like a slow Simple backwards, but Arbeau gives another which is more difficult.

Bar. Beat.

1   1 Raise the right foot forward and shake the toes lightly from side
     2   to side.

2   1
     2 Step on the right in third position, behind.

3   1 Raise the left forward, shaking the toes.
     2 Step on the left in third position, behind.

4   1 Raise the right forward, shaking the toes.
     2 Step on the right in third position, behind.

At Queen Elizabeth's Court the Pavane was usually danced by the older people ; it was dignified rather than elaborate. Costumes were stiffened and padded and it was more convenient to make the steps straight forward, without bowing to the side.

BOW AND COURTESY.

English fashions followed the French, rather than the Italian style, therefore the French bow and courtesy will be most suitable.
Bow.
To agree with the dance the bow must be made in the time of eight bars of duple time *(count eight slowly)*.
Count four.
Take off the hat with the left hand and carry it to the side with the inside of the hat towards the thigh. At the same time step back with the right foot to fourth position, where the right knee bends as it takes the weight. The bow is directed mainly to the audience, but you make a slight turn to include your partner.
Second count of four.
Rise, closing the right foot to first position and facing forward. Put on the hat, kiss your right hand and offer it to the lady.
COURTESY.
The lady keeps her feet in first position ; she must bend both knees equally, keeping them well turned out ; then rise smoothly. The lady must take her time from her partner, and make her movements agree with his. Unless in the presence of Royalty, the courtesy would not be very low.

Having risen from her courtesy, the lady waits for the gentleman to offer his hand, kisses her own finger tips, and places her hand in his.

EXAMPLE XII (b)

AN ENGLISH PAVANE.

Partners stand side by side, the lady on the right.   Bow and Courtesy.

Bars 1 and 2.   Simple to left, with slight bow forward as the right foot is closed.
Bars 3 and 4.   The same to the right, with contrary feet.
Bars 5 to 8.   Double forward with the left, well drawn up on the toes.
Bars 9 to 12.   Repeat bars 1 to 4, but begin to the right.
Bars 13 to 16. Reprise.

To complete the dance, these steps are performed four times (the music twice through).

At the end of the dance the same bow and courtesy should be made, but before replacing his hat the gentleman steps up to his partner, puts his right arm round her shoulder and his left hand (holding his hat) on her waist in front, and kisses her cheek.

STEPS USED IN THE GALLIARD

RÉVÉRENCE.

The Révérence should be the same that was used for the Pavane.

DOUBLES.

When Doubles were used they were the plain ones ; one step to each of the first three bars, closing the rear foot on the fourth bar.

True Galliard steps need two bars of triple time, like the Branle Gai or the Tordion, making a spring on each of the first four beats, and a Cadence for the last two.   This was called a Galliard Passage, and it was a strict rule that any Passage danced beginning with one foot must be repeated beginning with the other foot ; so every Passage was danced twice.

(a) PASSAGE CALLED " PIEDS CROISÉS."

Bar. Beat.

Bar	Beat	
1	1	Spring on the left foot, crossing the right in front, as in the Highland Fling.
	2	Spring on the right foot, crossing the left.
	3	Spring on the left foot, crossing the right.
2	1	Spring on the right foot, crossing the left.
	2	Spring on to the left foot, drawing it back.
	3	Point the right in front, on the ground.

$\left.\begin{array}{c} \\ \\ \end{array}\right\}$ Cadence.

Now you are ready to begin the repeat with the right foot.

This can also be danced turning, by making a quarter turn on each spring.

(b) Passage Called "Cinque Passi" or "Five Steps."

Bar. Beat.

1   1   Hop on the right, raising the left leg and right arm forward, swing the left arm back.

    2   Hop on the right, swinging the left leg and right arm back, and the left arm forward.

    3   Spring on to the left foot, raising the right leg forward, the arms do not change.

2   1   Spring on to the right foot, raising the left leg and right arm forward, swinging the left arm back.

    2   Spring on to the left foot, drawing it back.   } Cadence.

    3   Leave the right pointed in front, on the ground.

For the Cadence the arms come down by the sides.

It is important to remember that the arm movements were made to help the dancer's balance ; therefore they must always agree with the swing of the leg. Never make a big arm movement with a small swing of the leg.

Remember, too, that both leg and arm must swing easily, and not be put stiffly into position. This applies to all Passages.

"Cinque Passi Intrecciati." (Five steps interlaced.)

Bar. Beat.

1   1   Spring on to the left foot, crossing the right behind, as in the Highland Fling.

    2   Hop on the left, crossing the right in front.

    3   Hop on the left, stretching the right straight back.

2   1   Spring on to the right, raising the left forward.

    2   Spring on to the left, drawing it back.   } Cadence.

    3   Leave the right pointed in front, on the ground.

Passi Larghi in Gagliarda. (Slow Galliard Steps.).

Bar. Beat.

1   1   Rise on left toes, taking the right foot behind the left knee, keeping the right knee turned out. Both arms to left.

    2   Lower left heel, putting right foot down in third position behind.

    3   Rise on right toes, taking the left foot behind the right knee, keeping the left knee turned out. Both arms to right.

2   1   Lower right heel, putting down the left foot in third position behind.

    2   Raise left foot forward, but immediately spring on to it, drawing it back.

    3   Leave right foot pointed in front, on the ground. (For the last two bars, which are the Cadence, the arms should be by the sides with elbows turned out.)

It would not have been thought polite for a lady to make any strong movements ; besides, Sixteenth-century ladies wore heavy clothes padded and puffed ; so their movements were small and gentle. This would probably not apply to

Queen Elizabeth when she danced " six or seven galliards every morning " for exercise ; but she did that in her private apartments.

Here are passages suitable for ladies only.

Bar. Beat.

1	1	Rise on the toes and step to second position with the left.
	2	Close the right to first position, and lower the heels.
	3	Small spring to second on the left, raising right slightly in front.
2	1	Small spring to second on the right, raising the left slightly in front.
	2	Spring on to the left, drawing it back. ⎤
	3	Leave the right pointed in front on the ground. ⎦ Cadence.

A second passage for a lady.

Bar. Beat.

1	1	Spring on to the left, and step forward quickly with the right.
	2	Close the left in third position behind, raising the right forward.
	3	Spring on to the right, and step forward quickly with the left.
2	1	Close the right in third position behind, raising the left forward.
	2	Spring on to the left, drawing it back. ⎤
	3	Leave the right pointed in front on the ground. ⎦ Cadence.

The lady could do the " Five Steps " if she made them very small, and never lifted her foot more than a few inches from the ground.

When a lady and gentleman danced a Galliard they usually took it in turns to dance a passage, and the one who was not dancing promenaded in front of the dancer. The real business of a lady in dancing the Galliard was first, to admire whatever the gentleman did ; and second, to dance herself and give him time to get his breath for his next passage.

EXAMPLE XIII

GALLIARD TO BE DANCED BY A LADY AND GENTLEMAN.

Partners stand side by side, and begin exactly as they did in the Pavane, making the Révérence, and taking hands ; but in this case the Révérence will be part of the dance because more is made of it.

Bar. Beat.

1	1	
	2	
	3	
2	1	
	2	
	3	Révérence.
3	1	
	2	
	3	
4	1	
	2	
	3	

Bar.	Beat.	
5	1	
	2	
	3	
6	1	
	2	Double forward. In the last bar they release hands and the gentleman
	3	makes a half-turn, stepping back with his right foot instead of
7	1	closing it.
	2	
	3	
8	1	
	2	
	3	

9	1	They take left hands, first kissing their own hand.
	2	
	3	
10	1	
	2	
	3	Révérence. (The gentleman must take off his hat with his right
11	1	hand, and step back with the right foot.)
	2	
	3	
12	1	
	2	
	3	

13	1	
	2	
	3	
14	1	
	2	
	3	Double. (Gentleman goes back, lady forward, both make a half-turn
15	1	at the end to face each other.)
	2	
	3	
16	1	
	2	
	3	

Whilst the gentleman dances his Passages, the lady does four Doubles—one left and one to the right, followed by one to the right and one to the left.

Bar.	Beat.	
1	1	
	2	
	3	Gentleman alone. " Pieds croisés," beginning with the left.
2	1	
	2	
	3	
3	1	
	2	
	3	Gentleman alone. " Pieds croisés," beginning with the right.
4	1	
	2	
	3	
5	1	
	2	
	3	Gentleman alone. " Pieds croisés," turning to left.
6	1	
	2	
	3	
7	1	
	2	
	3	Gentleman alone. " Pieds croisés," turning to right.
8	1	
	2	
	3	

The gentleman will now do four Doubles to left and right.

9	1	
	2	
	3	Lady alone. First Passage, beginning with left.
10	1	
	2	
	3	
11	1	
	2	
	3	Lady alone. First Passage, beginning with right.
12	1	
	2	
	3	
13	1	
	2	
	3	Lady alone. Repeat first Passage, beginning with left.
14	1	
	2	
	3	

15   1 ⎫
      2 ⎪
      3 ⎬ Lady alone. Repeat first Passage, beginning with right.
16   1 ⎪
      2 ⎪
      3 ⎭

The lady does four Doubles, left and right.

Bar. Beat.

1   1 ⎫
    2 ⎪
    3 ⎬ Gentleman alone. " Cinque Passi Intrecciati." Begin left.
2   1 ⎪
    2 ⎪
    3 ⎭

3   1 ⎫
    2 ⎪
    3 ⎬ Gentleman alone. " Cinque Passi Intrecciati." Begin right.
4   1 ⎪
    2 ⎪
    3 ⎭

5   1 ⎫
    2 ⎪
    3 ⎬ Gentleman alone. " Cinque Passi Intrecciati." Turning left.
6   1 ⎪
    2 ⎪
    3 ⎭

7   1 ⎫
    2 ⎪
    3 ⎬ Gentleman alone. " Cinque Passi Intrecciati." Turning right.
8   1 ⎪
    2 ⎪
    3 ⎭

The gentleman will now do four Doubles to left and right.

Bar. Beat.

9   1 ⎫
    2 ⎪
    3 ⎬ Lady alone does her second Passage, beginning with left.
10   1 ⎪
    2 ⎪
    3 ⎭

Bar	Beat	
11	1	
	2	
	3	Lady alone does her second Passage, beginning with right.
12	1	
	2	
	3	
13	1	
	2	
	3	Lady alone repeats her second Passage, beginning with left.
14	1	
	2	
	3	
15	1	
	2	
	3	Lady alone repeats her second Passage, beginning with right.
16	1	
	2	
	3	

Bars 9-14 carry the lady towards her partner. On bars 15-16 she turns to place herself beside him as at the beginning. Finish with Bow, Curtsy and Kiss as in the Pavane.

EXAMPLE XIII (A)

GALLIARD ARRANGED AS SOLO FOR GENTLEMAN.

The Galliard, being a social dance, was really for two dancers; but it was a show dance, and there may have been occasions when it was danced as a solo. The Italian bow is given in this instance. Stand facing the audience, in the first position. Take off your hat with the left hand; hold it beside your knee, the inside of the hat towards you. The bow is made in the music of the dance.

	Bar.	Beat.	
	1	1	Draw back the left foot until the toe is level with the right heel, keeping the left heel on the ground, and
		2	the weight on the front foot. Incline the shoulders slightly, but keep the head up.
		3	
	2	1	Bend both knees a little, keeping them turned out.
		2	
Riverenza.		3	
	3	1	Straighten the knees and the body.
		2	
		3	
	4	1	Close the left foot to first position, and put on hat.
		2	
		3	

Continenza.	5	1	Small step with left foot to second position, drawing back the left shoulder.
		2	
		3	Rise on the toes, closing the right foot to first position.
	6	1	Lower the heels, bringing the shoulder level.
		2	
		3	

Continenza.	7	1	Small step with right foot to second position, drawing back the right shoulder.
		2	
		3	Rise on the toes, closing the left foot to first position.
	8	1	Lower the heels, bringing the shoulder level.
		2	
		3	

Bars 9-10. Cinque Passi Intrecciati, beginning with the left.
Bars 11-12. Cinque Passi Intrecciati. beginning with the right.
Bars 13-14. Cinque Passi Intrecciati, turning to the left.
Bars 15-16. Cinque Passi Intrecciati, turning to the right.

Bars 1- 2. Slow Galliard step, taking right back first.
Bars 3- 4. Slow Galliard step, taking left back first.
Bars 5- 6. Slow Galliard step, taking right back first.
Bars 7- 8. Slow Galliard step, taking left back first.

B. Bars 9-10. " Pieds Croisés," beginning with spring on left.
Bars 11-12. " Pieds Croisés," beginning with spring on right.
Bars 13-14. " Pieds Croisés," turning to left.
Bars 15-16. " Pieds Croisés," turning to right.

A. Bars 1- 2. Slow Galliard step, taking right back first.
Bars 3- 4. Slow Galliard step, taking left back first.
Bars 5- 6. Slow Galliard step, taking right back first.
Bars 7- 8. Slow Galliard step, taking left back first.

B. Bars 9-10. Cinque Passi, hop on left first.
Bars 11-12. Cinque Passi, hop on right first.
Bars 13-14. Cinque Passi, hop on left first.
Bars 15-16. Cinque Passi, hop on right first.

This is the end of the dance, so the gentleman takes off his hat and makes a slow bow as at the beginning, but without any music.

Example XII (b)

PAVANE
"La Traditore my fa morire"

Arranged by Elsie Palmer

Example XIII and XIII (a)

GALLIARD
"La Traditore my fa morire" from Arbeau's "Orchésographie"

Arranged by Elsie Palmer

Example XIV

B.M. MS. Add. 29485

LORAYNE ALMAIN

Original Harmonies

STEPS USED IN THE ALMAIN

ALMAIN DOUBLE.

Bar. Beat.

1   1   Step forward with the left.

      2

      3   Step forward with the right.

      4

2   1   Step forward with the left.

      2

      3   Hop on left, raising the right knee forward, right toe turned out and slightly pointed.

      4

ORDINARY DOUBLE.

Bar. Beat.

1   1   Step forward with the left, on the toes.

      2

      3   Step forward with the right, on the toes.

      4

2   1   Step forward with the left, on the toes.

      2

      3   Close right to first position, and lower the heels.

      4

REPRISE.

Bar. Beat.

1   1   Step back with the right on the toes.

      2

      3

      4   Draw the left foot back to first position, slowly.

2   1

      2

      3   Lower the heels.

      4

It should be noted that the Almain is the only dance (until the end of the Eighteenth Century) in which the hands are held high. Partners stand close beside each other, and after taking hands in the usual way, the arms are raised forwards to about shoulder level.

EXAMPLE XIV

Lorayne Almain. (From Bodleian MS., Rawl. Poet. 108.).

A. 1.

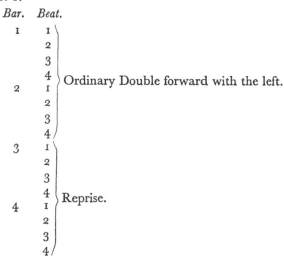

Bar. *Beat.*

1	1	
	2	
	3	
	4	Almain Double forward with the left.
2	1	
	2	
	3	
	4	
3	1	
	2	
	3	
	4	Almain Double forward with the right.
4	1	
	2	
	3	
	4	

A. 2.

Repeat these Two Almain Doubles.

B. 1.

Bar. *Beat.*

1	1	
	2	
	3	
	4	Ordinary Double forward with the left.
2	1	
	2	
	3	
	4	
3	1	
	2	
	3	
	4	Reprise.
4	1	
	2	
	3	
	4	

115

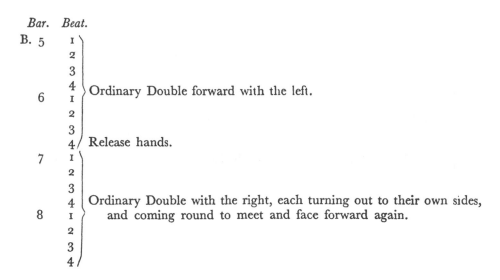

Bar. Beat.

B. 5 1 ⟩
      2 |
      3 |
6   4 ⟩ Ordinary Double forward with the left.
      1 |
      2 |
      3 |
      4 ⟩ Release hands.
7   1 ⟩
      2 |
      3 |
      4 | Ordinary Double with the right, each turning out to their own sides,
8   1 ⟩   and coming round to meet and face forward again.
      2 |
      3 |
      4 ⟩

B. 2.

Repeat the Last Eight Bars.

In the repeat of the Almain the steps are the same, but we are told to begin with eight Almain Doubles instead of four. This means that the A section of the music must be played four times before going on to the second section.

Historical Notes

17th Century

The first quarter of the Seventeenth Century was an epilogue to the Elizabethan period. Costume did not change materially ; people still ate with their fingers ; the Great Hall remained the centre of activity in a large house, though the family might live in more comfortable rooms built out from it.

There was a decline in general social dancing because the Court concentrated on the production of Masques. Elaborate spectacles had been produced in Italy even in the Fifteenth Century ; Catherine di Medici encouraged Ballets at the French Court in the Sixteenth Century ; but the Seventeenth-century English Court Masque was different, in that it was founded on Medieval Disguisings and Mummings. In the early form of courtly " Disguising " a stage was wheeled into the Great Hall. This stage might represent a mountain, or a cave, or some such fancy, and on it the performers were grouped. At a suitable moment they came down from their stage to show a specially prepared dance ; after which they sometimes took partners from the audience for ordinary social dancing. There is an example of this in Shakespeare's " Henry VIII " (Act I, Scene 4) where the king comes to Wolsey's feast with a party of Mummers, and afterwards dances with Anne Boleyn.

The Seventeenth-century Court Masque borrowed its stage settings, effects, machines and transformation scenes from Italy. In respect of these things the Masque was far in advance of the Theatre, which was still limited to the Elizabethan type of stage.

Masques followed a set formula. There was always some central idea—hardly amounting to a plot—to connect the various " entries." First there would be an entry for the noble performers in magnificent costume ; after songs and set speeches a ballet was danced, after which the masquers withdrew to change their costumes. The Anti-Masque followed, a comic or grotesque interlude provided by comics from the professional theatre.

Until the second half of the century there were no professional dancers except the comics, who performed Morris dances, Mattachins (sword dances), Galliards and jigs. Grotesque dances would have been beneath the dignity of courtiers, and equally no actor of that time would aspire to the " noble " style of dancing.

A second entry for the courtiers came next. The number of entries varied, but they were always divided by Anti-masques. Sometimes the design of the old Disguising was preserved by inserting a period of general dancing in which the Masquers took partners from the audience. This was called Commoning, or Communing. In any case there was always a final dance for the Masquers leading to their exit.

The best talent available was employed in the Masques. The script would be devised and written by Ben Jonson, or Samuel Daniel; Inigo Jones designed most of the costumes and settings; the music was by composers like Ferrabosco and Robert Johnson.

In the year 1604, Anne of Denmark celebrated her first Christmas in England with a Masque which was danced at Hampton Court. It was written by Samuel Daniel, and was called "The Vision of Twelve Goddesses." Here is a short account of the dances, taken from Daniel's preface to the printed edition of the text.

The Twelve Goddesses impersonated by the Queen and her ladies, had descended from a mountain and

> ". . . returned down into the midst of the hall, preparing themselves to their dance which . . . they began to the music of the Violls and Lutes, placed on one side of the Hall.
>
> "Which dance being performed with great majesty and Arte, consisting of divers straines, fram'd unto motions circular, square, triangular, with other proportions exceeding rare and full of variety; the Goddesses made a pause, casting themselves into a circle, whilst the Graces againe sang to the musicke of the Temple, and prepared to take out the lords to dance. With whom, after they had performed certain Measures, Galliards, and Curantos, Iris againe comes and gives notice of their pleasure to depart: whose speech ended, they drew themselves again into another short dance, with some few pleasant changes, still retyring them towards the foot of the Mountain, which they ascended in that same manner as they came down. . . ."

Here we find Measures of two kinds—the Measures danced by the Masquers alone, which were figure dances; and the Measures they danced with members of the audience which were more likely processional like the "Earl of Essex his Measures." The other dances were Galliards and Corantos, all late Elizabethan dances. There was no material change before 1623.

"The Vision of Twelve Goddesses" was the first of the series of Court Masques, and it kept closely to the old design. The Mountain was a fixture instead of being mounted on a cart, but there was only one main dance for the Masquers, and no Anti-masque; the Communing was retained, and there was a final dance for the general exit.

The reign of James I was the heyday of the "Italianate Englishman." Whilst there is still no evidence of the use of Italian dances, it is possible that the Measures made use of Italian steps, because the Royal Library at the British Museum contains a copy of Fabritio Caroso's "Nobilità di Dame," whose binding shows the Prince of Wales' coat-of-arms. This book is full of human interest because its pages are seriously stained with water, and one is reminded of Bulstrode Whitlocke's distress when he visited St. James' Palace during the Commonwealth and found the royal books scattered on the floor whilst rain poured in through broken windows. Whitlocke was a friend of Oliver Cromwell, and exerted all his influence to get the books moved to Whitehall; he was also a good dancer, as we will have occasion to see presently.

In 1625 Charles I succeeded his father, and in the same year he married Henrietta Maria, sister of the French king Louis XIII. From this time the Italianate Englishman who had annoyed the moralists was out of date, and French fashions were all the mode. We can appreciate the change at a glance by comparing portraits of James I and his Queen with those of Charles I and Henrietta Maria. Over decoration, false hair, farthingales, hip-cushions, ruffs and padded breeches, have all been abandoned ; their place is taken by simple and graceful dresses made of plain satin in soft colours, set off by falling collars of fine lace, and only one or two jewels.

It was the real beginning of life as we have known it. The change went far beyond costume, and embraced every part of social life. In the past, Courtesy books had been written for the instruction of children, and were concerned chiefly with the service and eating of meals. This was all important when meat had to be taken cleanly with the fingers. From the Seventeenth Century onwards we find instead, Civility Books written for adults ; and containing all that is necessary for an aspiring young man to know when he waits upon a " Person of Quality " whom he wishes to impress with his delicate attentions. By this time meals were served to the family apart from the household, and forks came into general use. New houses were no longer built round Great Halls, though they nearly always included a Long Gallery.

The change was no less marked in dancing. A completely fresh start was made by returning to the Suite of Branles, but they were not the old Branles. The suite began now with Branle Simple,[1] in a new form adapted for dancing to eight-bar phrases ; Branle Gai, no longer springing, but demanding the maximum of rise and fall over a controlled instep ; the Branle de Poitou reduced from a music-unit of six bars to one of four bars, and incorporating the serpentine figure from the old Farandole ; lastly, the Branle Double de Poitou. In England these were known collectively as the French Branles or the Brantle.

The Gavottes, which became prominent, were Branles Doubles in which each couple in turn took the centre and performed alone. The popularity of the dance lay in the fact that after their solo the gentleman kissed all the ladies, and his partner did the same for the gentlemen. Gavottes were progressive, but not in the English Country Dance meaning of the term. The top couple did not work their way down the dance, but after the interlude of kissing they took the lowest place and the next couple led.

The Galliarde was only a shadow of its former self, with springs reduced to instep movements, except in the case of a mild half-caper. It was soon forgotten.

The characteristic dance of the Seventeenth Century was the " Courante," which had become slow and dignified, though it retained its form as a progress round the room, partners pausing from time to time to face each other and perform various passages. In its final form the " Courante " was a connoisseur's dance ; the better the performance, the simpler, and therefore the duller it appeared ; it was carried off by the superb dignity of dancers like Louis XIV of France and our own Charles II. The " Courante " died out during the second half of the

[1] Example XVII, p. 136.

119

century, when it was gradually replaced by the "French Dances" to be described presently.

For our knowledge of these dances we are indebted to a book called "Apologie de la Danse," by F. de Lauze, published in England in 1623. Fortune did not smile on M. de Lauze. In the first place a false friend, to whom he had lent the manuscript, tried to bring out a version of his own in advance. This plan was defeated, as de Lauze tells us in his preface, because he had only lent the first half of the book, dealing with dancing for gentlemen. The second half, devoted to dancing for ladies, he had retained, and was therefore able to prove authorship. The MS. of the pirated version is in the British Museum.

When the book came out in 1623 it was dedicated to the Duke and Duchess of Buckingham. At that time the Duke was all powerful, the King's favourite ; but as he was assassinated the following year, the dedication cannot have been of much value to de Lauze.

These dances, with the English Country Dances, were used in England until some time after the restoration of Charles II. Only the Galliard seems to have been dropped immediately.

It is a mistake to suppose there was no dancing in England during the Civil War and the Commonwealth. A noisy minority of kill-joys would have liked to spoil everyone's pleasure, but they were only successful in respect of dancing round Maypoles. There must have been many families who did not wish to take any part in civil strife, and who stayed quietly at home hoping to keep out of trouble.

There is ample evidence to show that dancing was actively and openly practised. Sir Francis Throckmorton going to Cambridge, and later to Oxford in the Sixteen-fifties, made immediate arrangements with a dancing master. (" A Seventeenth-century Country Gentleman," E. A. B. Barnard ; Cambridge, 1944.)

Bulstrode Whitelocke, Cromwell's personal friend, and his Ambassador to Sweden in 1654, was the hero of a revealing story. Queen Christina had been told that no gentlemen remained in England, since all were exiled with the King in Holland. In order to test the truth of this statement, the Queen asked the Ambassador to dance with her at a ball. He would have excused himself, but she insisted. Whitelocke danced well, and the Queen thereupon declared she had been misinformed because any man who could dance must be a gentleman, and must have received a gentleman's education.

Nor must we forget the grand ball given by Cromwell himself for his daughter's wedding, when no less than fifty violins played for the dancing.

And there was John Playford. The publication of " The English Dancing Master " from 1651 onwards would be senseless if there were no social dancing ; but the production of a book which could be circulated throughout the kingdom answers to the prevailing conditions, in which many people stayed at home in the country and were cut off from the dancing schools.

It is proposed to treat the English Country Dance in some detail, because to so many people it means something one does at school, or with the Girl Guides ; something too often taught by the games' mistress or the gym. teacher, and hardly to be reckoned as real dancing. Nothing could be farther from the truth. Rooted in the English countryside, brought to Queen Elizabeth's Court where its development started, the Country Dance and the Measures were regarded as the characteristic English dances. The disturbed conditions during the Civil War and the Commonwealth favoured the growth of a domestic style ; therefore we find the Rounds for as many as will—which were out-of-door dances—tended to die out. At first there was an increase in the Long for eight, or Long for six, and Square for eight or four, all of which fit comfortably into rooms of moderate size. The Longways for as many as will progressive dance fitted the Long Gallery, which was a feature of most Seventeenth-century country houses.

Apart from the few kissing dances, English Country Dances have a delightfully impersonal character, which encouraged good dancing and made it possible to call in the servants to make up a set. It should never be forgotten that the existence of rigid distinctions made it easier for the classes to mix happily ; they were not divided by a layer of folk aspiring to the higher class whose traditions they had not learned, and despising the lower class to which they rightly belonged. Neither was there any self-conscious difference between town and country. Towns were smaller and town dwellers took their ease in the country without the need of a motor car to transport them. The country folk, for their part, were often in town ; they brought their produce direct to the consumer, and they either copied or derided town fashions as the humour took them. In any case, they all used the same dances. The grand Court Dances were excepted ; they were not for everyday use.

The first collection of Country Dances was " The English Dancing Master," published by John Playford in 1651. About sixty years had elapsed since Queen Elizabeth's Maids-of-Honour began to dance country dances at Court. How far are Playford's dances either " English " or " country " ? It is fair to say that basically they are both ; but some of them may have been altered by dancing masters, and some are certainly new dances composed by masters in the traditional idiom.

What was this traditional idiom ? What dances were in use before Playford began his collection ? Nashe in " Have with you to Saffron Walden " gives a list of dances seen at an average village merry-making : " Rogero, Basilena, Turkeyloney, All Flowers of the Broom, Pepper is Black, Greensleeves, Peggy Ramsey." Of these, " Roger " may be found in " The English Dancing Master " for 1695, and " Greensleeves " in the 1686 edition : these are late dates, and whilst it is possible the dances may have been altered in the meantime, it is not certain. " All Flowers of the Broom " must also be assigned to Playford, if it is the same as " Broom, Broom, the Bonny, Bonny Broom " given in the first edition. " Pepper is Black " is given in the first edition of 1651, and it has the appearance of an old dance.

The air of " Turkeyloney[1] " is found in William Ballett's Lute Book ; it was used for several dances :

(1) Dance called " Turkeyloney " in MSS. B.M. Harley 367 and Bodleian Douce 280. This is an Estampie Double (see p. 21).

[1] Example XV., p. 127.

(2) Dance called " Turkeyloney " in MS. Bodleian Rawl. Poet. 108. An Estampie Simple, with the Simple lengthened into a Reprise to fit the four-bar phrase.

(3) As an alternative air for " Tinternel," another dance in Estampie form occurring in all three MSS.

Three basic features of the English Country Dance are present in these dances :

(*a*) A Double forward and a Double back.

(*b*) Simple left and Simple right ; a movement of courtesy later known as Setting.

(*c*) A figure found in " Tinternel," in which partners take right hands to go round each other, than change hands to go back again. On the village green this might easily be danced by linking arms, the familiar Arming of the Country Dancer.

" Basilena " is also in Estampie form ; it combines Estampie Double with Estampie Simple. " Basilena " is only found in Bodleian MS Douce 280, but it is mentioned in a list of dances of Henry VIII's time.

There is more information about early country dances in Sir John Davies' poem " Orchestra," written in 1595, about the time when country dancing came to Court. Stanza LXIII is a fanciful description of a Farandole ending in a Round :

" As when a nymph arysing from the land.
Leadeth a daunce with her long watery traine
Downe to the Sea, she wries to every hand,
And every way doth crosse the fertile plaine :
But when at last she falls into the Maine,
Then all her traverses concluded are,
And with the Sea her course is circulare."

Here we have a linked dance pursuing a serpentine course, and finally joining to form a Round. This form is still used by Swedish folk dancers, with this exception : when the circle is formed, but before it is joined, they Thread the Needle several times. This is of interest because our own Rounds show traces of Threading the Needle in their figures.

Stanza LXIV deals more comprehensively with country dances :

" Thus when at first Love had them marshalled,
As erst he did the shapeless mass of things,
He taught them rounds and winding heyes to tread,
And about trees to cast themselves in rings :
As the two Beares, whom the First Mover flings
With a short turn about heaven's axel tree,
In a round daunce for ever wheeling bee."

Sir John Davies is very exact here, in drawing a distinction between Rounds and Ring dances : our circle dances have two forms :

(1) The Rounds, in which a simple figure is danced progressively round the circle. The figures often show traces of Threading the Needle, and seem to belong to a Farandole with the serpentine figure left

out. They are rightly linked with the Hey, which was also connected with the Farandole. When two lines met they might interlace before going their separate ways : or a single line might turn back upon itself as in the English dance " Dargason."

(2) Dances in which the movement implies some central object towards which advances are made. Sellenger's Round, associated with the maypole, has a recurring advance followed by a retreat and the " Setting " movement of courtesy.

All these dances belonged to the open air ; at Court they came within doors and, as it had happened earlier in Italy under similar circumstances, they quickly became figure dances. The disturbed conditions in England during the Seventeenth Century favoured the development of domestic dancing ; the dances in the early editions of " The English Dancing Master " will be found to fit comfortably into the average rooms of the period. Long Eights and Long Sixes for the larger rooms ; Square for Four where there was less space ; and Longways for as many as will for use in the Long Gallery that was a feature of so many country houses.

It should be noted in passing that the same considerations were in operation when country folk wanted to dance indoors. Their ballroom was usually the threshing floor of a barn, and these floors normally measured something in the neighbourhood of twenty feet by fourteen. The floor was either beaten earth or finely fitted boards.

In the course of time, when public Assemblies had largely replaced dancing at home, the Longways formation was the sole survivor.

Meanwhile matters had taken a different course in France. When Louis XIV ascended the throne in 1643, he was only five years old. The regency of his mother, Anne of Austria, and of Cardinal Mazarin was unpopular ; and, as in England, civil strife resulted. In 1651 Louis took over the government himself, and the most brilliant epoch in French history began. Louis was ambitious to shine in every kind of activity ; in dancing no less than in military adventures. He was an excellent dancer, and is said to have taken a lesson every day with the dancing master Beauchamps.

At first the young king satisfied his love of display by playing the leading part in magnificent Court Ballets ; but as he grew to manhood his advisers pointed out that a great king had a more important part to play on a larger stage. Louis was wise enough to take advice ; he danced no more Ballets, but he did not give up his interest in dancing.

From time immemorial, dancing masters had belonged to the minstrel's Guild of St. Julien. In 1661 Louis XIV incorporated them as an independent body called the " Académie Royale de Danse." The head of the new Academy was the king's master, Beauchamps. It seems probable that the " regulation " of the French dances and the standardisation of steps was the first work of the new Academy.

Our king Charles II spent much time at the French Court during his exile ; he was a notable dancer of the " Courante," and might therefore be expected to know all the latest developments ; nevertheless after his Restoration in 1660 the dances in use at the English Court were those made known by de Lauze in 1623. Pepys watched a Ball at Whitehall in 1662 which began with the Brantle (Branle):

> "After that the King led a lady a single Coranto; and then the rest of the lords, one after another, other ladies: very noble it was, and great pleasure to see. Then to country dances."

In 1666 Pepys was less easily pleased:

> "I also to the ball, and with much ado got up to the loft, where with much trouble I could see very well. . . . Presently after the King was come in, he took the Queene, and about fourteen more couple there was, and began the Branles, then to a Corant, and now and then a French dance; but that so rare that the Corants grew tiresome, that I wished it done."

In 1665 "The English Dancing Master" contained, in an appendix, a set of airs for various French dances; in 1666 they were still rare at the English Court; therefore it seems probable that they became fashionable in their new form soon after the foundation of the Académie Royale de Danse in 1661.

Probably the first dance to be regulated was the Minuet. In its original form as the Branle de Poitou, everything was left to the discretion of the gentleman leading the dance. Beauchamps regulated it by reducing it to a dance for one couple only, and controlling the figures by stating the number of steps to be taken. Henry Purcell wrote many Minuets, but most of them would be more properly called Branles de Poitou. His Branles de Poitou are written in eight-bar phrases; but at one point he began to write dances called New Minuet. The New Minuet and others of its class show an eight-bar phrase followed by one of twelve bars, as required by Beauchamps' regulated Minuet. The Duke of Monmouth danced a Minuet in the Masque of "Calisto Crowned" in 1675.

If "Macaulay's History" is to be believed, the Duke of Monmouth was a veritable ambassador of the Dance, because in 1685 he was teaching English Country Dances to the Court ladies in Holland.

Thus, three things happened in the Seventeenth Century that were to influence the whole course of dance history.

(1) The Académie Royal de Danse shaped the dances that would be used throughout the Eighteenth Century. We are accustomed to think of the Minuet as the typical Eighteenth-century dance; and so it was in so far as it displaced the "Courante"; but it should always be borne in mind that the Minuet was fashionable long before the end of the Seventeenth Century, and it was closely followed by the rest of the "French Dances" (the Bourrée, Passepied, Rigaudon, Loure, etc.).

(2) The Académie Royale de Danse began to train professional dancers (women as well as men) in the "noble" style of dancing which had hitherto been the preserve of courtly amateurs. The amateurs were not prepared to give up their supremacy without a struggle,

and the very peak of achievement in social dancing was reached in the early Eighteenth Century. The preparatory work, however, belonged to the Seventeenth Century.

(3) Side by side with these spectacular developments, the English Country Dance was shaped quietly and unobtrusively. Although the names of several dancing-masters can be associated with it, none of them claimed any outstanding part in its growth. It was typically English ; everyone contributed. By the end of the Seventeenth Century the English dances began to be appreciated on the Continent. Not unnaturally they met with shocked opposition from the great French masters. By the time the Eighteenth Century had run its course the French Dances were no more, but the English Country Dance remained ; it was our serious contribution to the History of Dancing.

Dances

17th Century

EXAMPLE XV

" TURKEYLONEY "
(From B.M. MS. Harley 367. f178)

STEPS USED IN " TURKEYLONEY "

DOUBLES.

Bar. Beat.

1	1	Step forward with the left on the toes.
	2	
	3	
	4	Step forward with the right on the toes.
	5	
	6	
2	1	Step forward with the left on the toes.
	2	
	3	
	4	Close the right to first position and lower the heels.
	5	
	6	

Doubles forward should be made as usual, but Doubles back with very small steps. If all Doubles were made in the same way the dance would stay in the same place. This is an advantage if you want to use it in a play, and the stage is small ; but " Turkeyloney " was used on the village green, and they would want to make it move.

SIMPLES.

All the Simples in " Turkeyloney " are made to the side, as in English Country Dance " setting."

Bar. Beat.

1	1	Step with the left to second position, on the toes.
	2	
	3	
	4	Close the right to first position, on the toes and lower heels.
	5	
	6	

126

Example XV

TURKEYLONEY

William Ballet's Lute Book. Trin. Coll. Dublin
Chappell. "Old English Popular Music" 1893. Vol.I, p. 237

Introduction

Example XVI

MILL-FIELD

Playford "The English Dancing-Master"

First Edition 1651

Arranged by Elsie Palmer

"Turkeyloney" used on the village green would begin with a bob curtsey from the girl and a small bow from the boy. If there were any important people watching, the bow and curtsy would be made to them. Partners stand side by side, the girl on the right, and take hands without raising them at all.

If "Turkeyloney" was danced at Court it would have the ceremonious bows and curtsies like other Court dances. The music has eight bars of introduction which could be used for this purpose.

If used as a Country dance it would be better to leave out the introduction. "Turkeyloney" can be danced to many old English airs ; "Greensleeves" fits it perfectly.

TURKEYLONEY.

A. 1.

Bar. Beat.

1	1	
	2	
	3	
	4	
	5	
	6	Double forward with the left.
2	1	
	2	
	3	
	4	
	5	
	6	

3	1	
	2	
	3	
	4	
	5	
	6	Double back with the right.
4	1	
	2	
	3	
	4	
	5	
	6	

A. 1.
Bar. *Beat.*

5	1 2 3 4 5 6	
6	1 2 3 4 5 6	Double forward with the left.

7	1 2 3 4 5 6	
8	1 2 3 4 5 6	Double back with the right.

A. 2.
Repeat these eight bars and four Doubles.

B. 1.
Bar. *Beat.*

1	1 2 3 4 5 6	Simple to the left.
2	1 2 3 4 5 6	Simple to the right.

B. 1.
Bar. *Beat.*

Bar	Beat	
3	1	
	2	
	3	
	4	
	5	
	6	Double forward with the left.
4	1	
	2	
	3	
	4	
	5	
	6	

B. 2.
Bar. *Beat.*

Bar	Beat	
1	1	
	2	
	3	
	4	
	5	
	6	Double back with the right.
2	1	
	2	
	3	
	4	
	5	
	6	
3	1	
	2	
	3	Simple to the left.
	4	
	5	
	6	
4	1	
	2	
	3	Simple to the right.
	4	
	5	
	6	

A. 1 AND A. 2.

Repeat the " Double forward, Double back " four times as at the beginning.

130

MILL FIELD

English Country Dance from "The English Dancing Master."
(Playford.) 1651

STEPS USED IN MILL FIELD

ORDINARY DOUBLES.

Bar.	Beat.		
I	I	Step forward with the left.	
	2		
	3		
	4	Step forward with the right.	
	5		
	6		
2	I	Step forward with the left.	Double.
	2		
	3		
	4	Close the right to first position, and	
	5	lower the heels.	
	6		

Remember that in a circle dance moving to the left is "forward" and to the right is "back." Always begin with the left in going forward.

SETTING.

Another name for the two Simples made to the side.

Bar.	Beat.		
I	I	Step with the left to second position.	
	2		
	3		Simple.
	4	Close the right to first position, and	
	5	lower the heels.	
	6		
2	I	Step with the right to second position.	
	2		
	3		Simple.
	4	Close the left to first position, and	
	5	lower the heels.	
	6		

TURN SINGLE.

This name is misleading because it sounds as if one should turn round with one single (or Simple). In the MSS descriptions of dances about this time we are told to "turn a Double round in place," and that is exactly what one does.

To "turn Single" probably means to turn by oneself, not taking hands or linking arms with anyone else.

EXAMPLE XVI

MILL FIELD.

This is a Round for as many as will, so everyone must take hands in a circle.

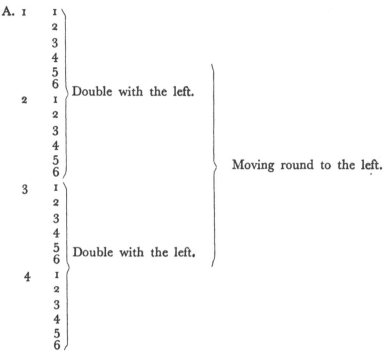

Bar. Beat.

A. 1 1 ⎫
      2 ⎪
      3 ⎪
      4 ⎪
      5 ⎪
      6 ⎬ Double with the left.
   2 1 ⎪
      2 ⎪
      3 ⎪
      4 ⎪
      5 ⎪
      6 ⎭   ⎬ Moving round to the left.
   3 1 ⎫
      2 ⎪
      3 ⎪
      4 ⎪
      5 ⎪
      6 ⎬ Double with the left.
   4 1 ⎪
      2 ⎪
      3 ⎪
      4 ⎪
      5 ⎪
      6 ⎭

A. 2.

Repeat these four bars, beginning the Doubles with the right, and moving round to the right. Release Hands.

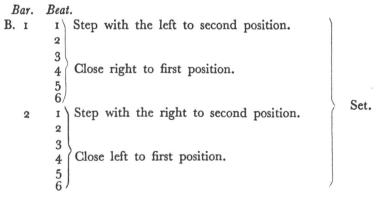

Bar. Beat.

B. 1 1 ⎫ Step with the left to second position.
      2 ⎪
      3 ⎪
      4 ⎬ Close right to first position.
      5 ⎪
      6 ⎭   ⎫
   2 1 ⎫ Step with the right to second position.   ⎬ Set.
      2 ⎪   ⎪
      3 ⎪   ⎭
      4 ⎬ Close left to first position.
      5 ⎪
      6 ⎭

132

A. 2.

Bar.	Beat.			
3	1	Step left.		
	2			
	3	Step right.		
	4			
	5			Double turning to the left in place.
	6			
4	1	Step left.		
	2			
	3	Close right.		
	4			
	5			
	6			

B. 2.

Repeat the last four bars, beginning with right and turning right.

Bar.	Beat.		
A. 1	1		
	2		
	3		
	4		
	5		
	6	Double with the left.	First couple make an arch and go towards the second man (who is on their right); at the same time, he comes towards them and passes under the arch.
2	1		
	2		
	3		
	4		
	5		
	6		
3	1		
	2		
	3		
	4		
	5		
	6	Double with left.	The first couple take both hands and go round.
4	1		
	2		
	3		
	4		
	5		
	6		

A. 2.

Repeat these four bars, the second man going under the arch again to his place. They finish in a triangle facing each other.

133

A. 2.

Bar. *Beat.*

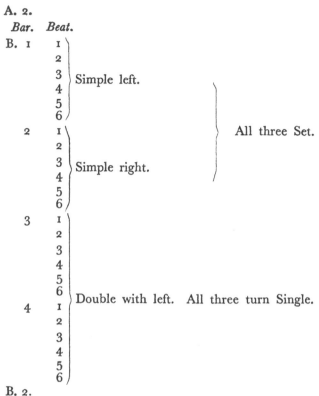

B. 1   1 ⎫
       2
       3 ⎬ Simple left.
       4
       5
       6 ⎭

  2   1 ⎫   All three Set.
       2
       3 ⎬ Simple right.
       4
       5
       6 ⎭

  3   1
       2
       3
       4
       5
       6 ⎬ Double with left. All three turn Single.
  4   1
       2
       3
       4
       5
       6 ⎭

B. 2.

Repeat the last four bars.

Bars 1-2.   As in the last figure, but this time the two men make the arch and the woman passes under it.

     3-4.   The two men link arms and go round.

In the repeat of these four bars the woman passes under the arch again to her place. The men link arms and go round again.

Bars 1-4.   All three Set and turn Single.

     1-4.   Set and turn Single again.

Bars 1-2.   This time the second man makes an arch with the first woman, and the first man passes under.

     3-4.   Second man and first woman take hands and go round.

In the repeat of these four bars the first man passes under the arch again to his place. The second man and first woman take hands and go round again.

Bars 1-2.   All three Set and turn Single.

     3-4.   Set and turn Single again.

So far all the dancing, after the Doubles round in a circle, has been done by the first couple and the second man. Now they begin again and do the three

Example XVII

BRANLE SIMPLE. 17th Century
"We be three poor Mariners"
from Chappell."Old English Popular Music"
Incorrectly given in Skene MS. as a Branle de Poitou

Example XVIII

**FOR BRANLE DE POITOU
MINUET**

PURCELL

arch figures with the second woman. Then the first goes on to do the three figures with each of the other dancers in turn, and when they have been all round the circle the dance is finished.

EXAMPLE XVII

Branle Simple. (De Lauze. 1623.).

This is Branle Simple adapted for use with music written in four-bar phrases ; the Simple has two steps added to make it as long as the Double. As the music is written in modern notation we take two steps to each bar, and the dance unit is completed in four bars. Although the steps are made in a more regulated style, the Branles were still informal dances ; there was no exact beginning or ending because people might join after the dance had started, provided they went to the last place on the line. People made their bows and curtsies, and picked up the music at the right moment. The dancing masters made the bows and curtsies as difficult as possible by putting in a number of small steps ; but we will make them as simple as we can.

Gentleman's Bow.

First take off the hat with the left hand.

Bar.	Beat.	
1	1	Small step to second position with the left foot.
	2	
	3	Step with the right to small fourth position behind.
	4	
2	1	Bend both knees slightly, keeping them turned out.
	2	
	3	Straighten the knees again.
	4	
3	1	Make a step with the right foot towards the lady, kissing your right
	2	hand and offering it to her.
	3	
	4	
4	1	Put on your hat.
	2	
	3	
	4	

The Lady's Curtsey.

Bar.	Beat.	
1	1	Small step to second position with the left foot.
	2	
	3	Glide the right forward to fourth position, with weight equally
	4	distributed.
2	1	Bend both knees slightly.
	2	
	3	Straighten the knees again.
	4	

3   1 Close the rear foot to first position.

     2

     3 When the gentleman offers his hand, the lady must kiss her left hand
     4   and place it in his.

4   1

     2

     3

     4

BRANLE SIMPLE.

Bar. Beat.

1   1 Make a circular step with the left to second position, keeping the
     2   heels on the ground.
     3 Bring the right foot to fifth position in front, well turned out.
     4

2   1 Left to second position, still keeping the heels on the ground.
     2
     3 Close right to first position, rising on the toes.
     4

3   1 Left to small second position on the toes.
     2
     3 Right to fifth position behind, on the toes, turning the body to the
     4   right.

4   1 Circular step with the left to second position, on the toes. Face
     2   forward again.
     3 Close the right and lower heels.
     4

This completes the dance-unit, which is repeated as often as the dancers wish.

EXAMPLE XVIII

BRANLE DE POITOU. (De Lauze. 1623.) (The Dance-Unit of the Seventeenth-
century Branle de Poitou.)

Bar. Beat.

1   1 Close the right to first position, rising on the toes.
     2 Step to small second position with left, on the toes.
     3 Right to fifth position in front, on the toes.

2   1 Left to second position, lower heels.
     2 Bend both knees very slightly in order to rise on the toes.
     3 Close right to first position, rising on the toes.

3   1 ⎫
   and ⎬ Four small running steps to left on the toes. Begin left.
     2 ⎪
   and⎭

     3 Left to second position, on the toes.

   4   1 Close right to first position, on the toes.

         2 Left to second position, lower heels.

         3 Bend both knees very slightly in order to rise on the toes, and begin again.

These steps are kept going throughout the dance ; but instead of dancing in a circle, as in most Branles, this one borrows the winding course of the Farandole.

The first gentleman leads his partner round to face the rest of the line, and as they are all holding hands, they follow in turn.

There is a particular way to hold hands in this dance. When the gentleman has kissed his hand and offered it to the lady, and she has kissed her hand and laid it on his, still holding her hand firmly he lifts it and rests his hand on his waist, turning it so that the knuckles are towards himself. The lady with her right hand must hold the right hand of the following gentleman in the same way. This means the dancers are closer together than is usual, and it is even more necessary for all of them to keep perfect time.

When the first lady and gentleman reach the end of the line, they must make a half turn to the left so their backs will be towards the rest of. the dancers, and because it is not easy to turn in such close formation, the gentleman was told to take his hand away from his waist whilst they were turning. He would do the same at the other end when they turn to face the line as at the beginning.

It might happen that the first couple wanted to stop dancing, but the others to keep on. In this case the lady must release the hand of the gentleman who follows her, her partner takes both her hands and moves backwards, drawing her away from the line to any part of the room where they can make their bow and curtsy without inconvenience to the dancers.

The bows and curtsies at the beginning and end of this Branle should be the same as those used for the Branle Simple (see p. 120).

Purcell wrote two kinds of Minuet. Some, which consist of two eight-bar phrases, belong to the Branle de Poitou which became the Minuet. Others, which consist of an eight-bar phrase and a twelve-bar phrase, are true Minuets and fit the dance as described by Rameau.

THE MINUET. (Steps used in the Minuet.)

All steps used in the Minuet begin with the right foot, in whichever direction one moves.

Although Minuet airs are always written in 3/4 time, it should really be 6/4, because we count six for each Minuet step.

The first movement, which is a slight bending of the knees (the dancers call it plié), is only a preparation for the step, so it is made on the last beat of the previous bar, and we really have to count 6, 1, 2, 3, 4, 5.

Bar. Beat.

        6 Bend the knees slightly.

  1   1 Step forward with the right, rising on the toes. Close L.

     and Lower the heels.

        2 Bend the knees slightly.

        3 Step forward with the left, rising on the toes. Close R.

Fig. VIII. BRANLE, 17TH CENTURY

From " The Dancing Lesson," by Mathieu Le Nain, 1607–1677

(Collection : Louis de Seyssel)

FIG. IX. STUDY FOR A MASKED BALL AT WANSTEAD ASSEMBLY, 18TH CENTURY
From the painting by William Hogarth, South London Art Gallery

Photo: A. C. Cooper.

FIG. X. ALLEMANDE, 18TH CENTURY
From the Engraving, 'Le Bal Paré," after Auguste de St. Aubin

2   1 Step forward with the right, on the toes.

     2 Step forward with the left, on the toes. Close R.

and Lower the heels.

3

The last beat belongs to the next step.

The steps must be small, because the important thing is to rise on the toes and come down again smoothly and in perfect time, and you cannot control your instep unless the weight of your body is right over the supporting foot. Remember then to take small steps, and keep the weight forward all the time.

Bar. Beat.

          Minuet step to the left.

     6 Bend the knees slightly.

1   1 Step with the right to the fifth position in front. Rising on the toes,

and   bring the left to first position. Lower the heel at once.

     2 Bend the knees slightly.

     3 Small step with the left to second position, rising on the toes.

2   1 Step with the right to fifth position behind, on the toes.

     2 Step with the left to small second position.

and   Lower the heel at once.

3

Bow and Curtsy.

Because we are talking about the Minuet, which lasted all through the Eighteenth Century, we will do the Eighteenth-century bows which were probably used in the late Seventeenth Century as well. Although they may sound complicated, they are really easy, and should be made without any fuss or flourishes.

Two bows were made, the first to the important people who were looking on, and the second turning to bow to each other.

When two people were going to dance they went to the middle of the room and stood side by side, the lady on the right, facing the audience, and pointing their inside foot.

The musicians played a flourish in the time of the dance, for bows.

The gentleman takes off his hat with the left hand and holds it beside him with the inside part forward. He makes a little movement with his right hand as if he might be going to kiss it, and offers it to the lady. She will place her left hand in his. That is the signal for the musicians to begin the flourish.

Bar.	Beat.	Gentleman.	Lady.
1	1	Draw the right foot back to a	Draw the left foot back to first
	2	small second position, and	position, bend both knees,
	3	bow from the waist.	keeping them turned out.
2	1	Close the left foot to first	Straighten the knees.
	2	position, straightening the	
	3	body.	

Now they must turn to face each other, and as this movement comes in the music of the flourish, there is less time left for the bow.

Bar.	Beat.	Gentleman.	Lady.
3	1	Step right to fifth position, in front.	Step left to fifth position, in front.
	2	Step left to second position, turning to face partner.	Step right to first position, turning to face partner.
	3	Bow.	Plié.
4	1	Straighten.	Straighten the knees, slowly.
	2		
	3	Put on hat.	

The Minuet given here is a Country Dance Minuet for as many as will, therefore the dancers may remain facing each other in two lines.

The True Minuet is too difficult for beginners.

EXAMPLE XIX

MINUET : " SABINA." (From " The English Dancing Master.")

Longways for as many as will. The dancers work in sets of four. The first and second couples take hands in a ring.

Bar. Beat.

A. 1	1
	2
2	3 } Minuet step to the left.
	1
	2
	3
3	1
	2
4	3 } Minuet step to the left.
	1
	2
	3
5	1
	2
6	3 } Minuet step to the left.
	1
	2
	3

Release hands.

7	1
	2
8	3 } Each makes a Minuet step, turning left in place.
	1
	2
	3

Take hands again.

A. 2.

Repeat bars 1-8, by which time all should be in their original places again. Now the first couple dances alone.

Bar. Beat.

B. 1   1
     2
     3 } Minuet step (forward), each turning out to their own side.
  2   1
     2
     3

  3   1
     2
     3 } Minuet step (forward), meeting below the third couple and taking
  4   1   both hands.
     2
     3

  5   1
     2
     3 } Two Minuet steps, going round to the left.
  6   1
     2
     3

  7   1
     2
     3 } Gentleman's right hand releases lady's left hand.
  8   1
     2
     3

B. 2.

Bar. Beat.

1   1
    2
    3
2   1
    2
    3 } Two Minuet steps leading down between the third couple, releasing
3   1   hands, and turning out between the third and fourth couples.
    2
    3
4   1
    2
    3

B. 2.

Bar. Beat.

5	1	
	2	
	3	
6	1	
	2	Two Minuet steps coming round between the second and third
	3	couples. Make a little bow to the second couple because you are
7	1	leaving them, and take hands in a ring with the third couple,
	2	ready to begin again from the beginning.
	3	
8	1	
	2	
	3	

During the next turn the second couple must stand still, because they have no one to dance with ; but when the first couple go on to dance with the fourth couple, the second and third couples begin to dance ; and so it goes on until everyone is dancing.

Example XIX

SABINA
Longways Minuet from "The English Dancing Master"

Arranged by Elsie Palmer

Historical Notes

18th Century

The Eighteenth Century reaped where the Seventeenth Century had sown.

In France, Louis XIV lived until 1715 ; he had established his court as the centre of Social life, and his successors maintained this tradition. Courtiers counted it exile worse than death, to be sent to live on their country estates.

In England there was a brief period of brilliance under Queen Anne ; but, with the exception of George IV, the Hanoverian kings never succeeded in giving a lead to Society : their traditions were alien, and their family discords created social confusion. Under these circumstances, the diffusion practised in the Seventeenth Century continued in the Eighteenth, though for a different reason.

The English nobility and gentry were happy to live on their estates, only coming to London to fulfil their Parliamentary duties, and to go to Court. The tenantry were often regarded as an extension of the family circle, and festivities at the big house, such as weddings, christenings, or the coming of age of the heir, were shared by all, forming a pleasant addition to the round of seasonal festivals. Country Dances more than held their own, though the young ladies and gentlemen practised their minuets for formal occasions.

Fashionable spas and watering places increased in importance, notably Bath, where the highest standards of dancing and deportment were demanded. At these resorts, dancing took place in large Assembly Rooms. The Longways progressive dance was the most popular because it enabled a great many couples to stand up together. Nevertheless a certain number of minuets were danced to open the ball.

Assemblies were not confined to Bath, or even to the most fashionable circles. Up and down the country every town, and many a village inn, had its Assembly Room which was used for private as well as public balls. By the mid-Eighteenth Century many people were living in comparatively small houses, and they found it convenient to join forces to hire the local Assembly Room when they wanted to dance.

The focal point of Court dancing, both in France and in England, was the King's Birthday Ball. A new dance was composed for this occasion by the Court dancing master ; it was printed in stenochoreographic notation for circulation to other dancing masters, and for sale to the public. Everyone who hoped to attend the Birthday Ball, or who wished other people to think they were going to attend the Ball, had to know the new dance ; and this arrangement was highly profitable to the dancing masters.

Feuillet's system of dance notation made it possible to record the dances in readily intelligible form, and we are able to re-create the compositions of great masters like Pécour with reasonable degree of accuracy. It cannot be stressed too often that the Eighteenth-century dances are individual creations composed by masters. Each is fitted to a particular piece of music so that, for example, one Bourrée cannot be danced to the music of another. This feature was exaggerated when several dances were combined in one. Pécour used this device in the Bourrée d'Achille, which has a central section in Minuet rhythm. L'Abbée's dances, composed for the English Court, are nearly all multiple forms : " Sarabande-Boree," " Rigodon-Passepied," " Chaconne-Hornpipe," and so on. There were also dances called " Branle," " Pavane," " Forlana," which have no more than a slender musical link with the original forms. All are elaborate figure dances for one couple alone, using the same rather limited range of steps. The dancer was expected to fit these steps to any musical rhythm.

The dances in general use were the Minuet, Bourrée, Passepied, Loure, Rigadoon, and Gavot, to which the Hornpipe must be added in England. (Perhaps it is necessary to say that there is no connection with " The Sailor's Hornpipe " of our children's dancing classes).

The Minuet stood alone. The Minuet had a pedigree reaching back to the Branle de Poitou. The Minuet had its own step and its own figure. The Minuet could be danced to any Minuet air. There was only one dance called THE MINUET ; this continued without modification until about 1765, when " a new way of dancing the Minuet " was introduced. Besides THE MINUET there were many Figured Minuets, composed freely in the same manner as the Bourrées, Passepieds, etc. There were also Country dances using Minuet steps and music, just as in the Nineteenth Century there were Waltz Country dances. The Minuet Country dances were in Longways progressive form ; they provide an opportunity to practise the steps without too much formality. (Example XIX, p. 140.)

The debutante's first ball must have been a terrible ordeal ; she had to stand up alone with her partner to dance her Minuet before the company ; conscious of the critical regard of her contemporaries and their parents. The standard young ladies were supposed to attain before leaving school can be seen from a book of dances put into stenochoreographic notation and published by Pemberton in 1711 ("An Essay for the Further Improvement of Dancing "). Here we have a Minuet for Four Ladies, and another for Three Ladies, with the figures drawn, but the steps merely indicated, it being left to the discretion of the dancing-master to use the full Minuet step, the more common simplified Minuet step, or any of the permitted variations, according to the proficiency of the pupils.

There is also a Solo Minuet, apparently intended as a test piece for the best pupil ; this dance provides a valuable study for anyone interested in the Minuet, because each figure offers some special technical difficulty.

Such, briefly, were the " French Dances " ; they had to face strong competition from the English Country Dances, which spread rapidly all over Europe. In the Eighteenth Century " Country Dance " meant Longways for as many as will progressive. Two features contributed to the enormous popularity of the English dances : first, there was the fact that any number of couples could stand

145

up at one time ; and secondly there was their truly sociable character, since every couple met and danced with every other couple in the course of the dance.

The old Simples and Doubles had, by this time, been replaced by more up-to-date steps. The following " steps that suit best with Country Dances " were given by John Essex in his " Chorography " (1710) :

" Gavot. (The Contretemps, see p. 156.)
" Drive Sideways. (Chassé, or Slip, see p. 156.)
" Bourrée. (One Demi-Coupé followed by two Pas Marchés.)
" Little Hops. (Skipping.)
" The Little Hops are more in fashion."

The French met the challenge of the English Country Dance by producing one of their own, called The Cotillon.[1] This Square-for-Eight figure dance enjoyed great popularity, especially in the second half of the century.

The Cotillon sometimes took on the character of the Allemande.[2] " To " Allemande " meant to interlace the arms in various ways, especially when each puts the left hand behind their own back, and with the right hand takes the left hand of their partner.[3] There is pictorial evidence to show that this method of interlacing the arms was used in the Sixteenth-century Almain, and this is the only apparent link between the two dances.[4] In the Eighteenth-century Allemande we also find the gentleman turning his partner under his arm, which suggests some borrowing from contemporary German folk-dance.[5]

At the end of the century the Cotillon, reduced to two couples, became the Quadrille, in which form it lasted until far into the Nineteenth Century. The various sets of Quadrilles were usually arranged in patterns on the dance floor. Sometimes two sets stood in a Square-eight formation, but they danced quite independently until the last figure when they joined in a chain or circular Hey.

To sum up. Such were the Eighteenth-century social dances. In the first quarter of the century they reached the peak of technical perfection, after which there was a decline. The Minuet held its unique place, but the Cotillons and Country Dances gained ground steadily. There were two reasons for this, and they were closely connected. Until the late Seventeenth Century anyone who wished to see the finest dancers of the day looked for them at Court ; but by the beginning of the Eighteenth Century the Académie Royale de Danse had a trained body of professionals—women as well as men—in the " noble " style of dancing which had not hithero been seen on the public stage. The courtly amateurs worked hard to maintain their supremacy ; but they could not compete seriously with people who were giving their whole time to the study and practice of their Art.

Pécour composed dances for both amateurs and professionals, and by comparing one style with the other we find that, in its beginning, the professional

[1] See p. 157, *et seq.* Example XXI
[2] Example XXII, p. 167.
[3] See Figure 10.
[4] See Figure 1. (Frontispiece).
[5] See Figure 10.

Ballet used the same steps as the ballroom dancers, but elaborated with many extra graces.

In time, Society gave up the unequal contest and relaxed, making use of the Cotillons and Country dances ; but the Minuet remained because it had become almost a ritual.

The French Revolution in 1790 extinguished the courtly style of dancing and deportment. Later, when Napoleon's Court scintillated with meretricious brilliance, there was no revival of aristocratic manners. Whereas under the old regime the gentleman took the lady's hand and led her—as our King still leads the Queen at the opening of Parliament and such formal occasions—now middle-class manners were the mode, and the lady slipped her hand through the gentleman's proffered arm. This note of familiarity was the death knell of the old order. The last ten years of the Eighteenth Century belong to the new world—our world—and they lie beyond the limits of these notes.

Dances

18th Century

EXAMPLE XX

LA GAVOTTE DU ROI. (Or the King's Gavotte.).
The King was Louis XV of France, who came to the throne in 1715. This dance was composed for him in 1716, when he was six years old.

STEPS.

The Honours. (Bow and Curtsey.)

Partners stand side by side, the lady on the right. As this dance is for two couples, they will stand facing each other at a distance of about four paces. The first Honour will be to the opposite couple, in the second partners Honour each other. All stand with the weight on the outside foot, the inside foot pointed in front. The gentlemen take off their hats with the left hand and hold them by the side ; they offer their right hand to the lady, who places her left hand on it. This is the signal for the musicians to begin the flourish.

Bar.	Beat	Gentlemen.	Ladies.
1	1	Draw back the right foot to second position.	Draw back the left foot to first position.
	2		
	3	Bow from the waist.	Bend both knees equally.
	4		
2	1	Rise from the bow.	Rise slowly.
	2		
	3	Close left foot to third position. behind.	
	4	(They release hands.)	
3	1	Step across with right to more than fifth position, in front.	Step across with left to more than fifth position in front.
	2	Step with left to second position, making quarter turn to face partner.	Step with right to second position, making quarter turn to face partner.
	3	Bow from the waist.	Bend both knees equally.
	4		

Example XX   "LA GAVOTTE DU ROI"

From Dezais Recüeil de Danses 1716

Arranged by Elsie Palmer

Bar.	Beat.	Gentlemen.	Ladies.
4	1	Rise from the bow.	Rise slowly.
	2		
	3	Close the right foot to third position behind.	Close the left foot to third position behind.
	4		
5	1	Step across with left to more than fifth position, in front.	Step across with right to more than fifth position, in front.
	2	Half turn left to face front, moving right to second position.	Half turn right to face front, moving left to second position.
	3	Step back with left to fourth position behind.	Step back with the right to fourth position behind.

Bars 6 *and* 7. The Gentlemen put on their hats.

Bar 8. The Gentleman offers his right hand to the Lady, who puts her left hand in it.

CONTRETEMPS.

Bar.	Beat.		
1	1	Hop on the left foot.	
	2	Step forward with the right on the toes.	
	3	Step forward with the left on the toes.	
	4		

You will find that Contretemps continue with the foot which began, therefore when you practise them you must do several beginning with one foot, then stop and begin again with the other foot.

In this dance every Contretemps is followed by an Assemblé, which was a spring closing the rear foot to first position. Sometimes this was followed by a walking step (Pas Marché) either forward or back. These are the only steps used throughout the dance, but at the very end there is another step called a Full Coupé which is more difficult.

FULL COUPÉ.

Bar.	Beat.		
	4	Bend both knees slightly.	
1	1	Step forward with the left, rising on the toes.	
	2	Slide the right forward to fourth position, on the toes.	
	3	Lower the right heel.	
	4		

LA GAVOTTE DU ROI. (Figure I.).

A. 1.

Bar.	Beat.	Gentlemen.	Ladies.
1	1	Contretemps forward. (Hop on right.)	Contretemps forward. (Hop on left.)
	2		
	3		
	4		

A. 1.

Bar.	Beat.	Gentlemen.	Ladies.
2	1	Assemblé, left to first position.	Assemblé, right to first position.
	2		
	3	Step back on right.	Step back on left.
	4		
3	1 ⎫		
	2 ⎬ Contretemps back.	Contretemps back.	
	3 ⎪ (Hop on right.)	(Hop on left.)	
	4 ⎭		
4	1	Assemblé, left to first position.	Assemblé, right to first position.
	2		
	3	Step forward on right.	Step forward on left.
	4		

A. 2.

Bar.	Beat.		
1	1 ⎫		
	2 ⎬ Contretemps forward.	Contretemps forward.	
	3 ⎪ (Hop on right.)	(Hop on left.)	
	4 ⎭		
2	1	Assemblé, left to first position, quarter turn to right.	Assemblé, right to first position, quarter turn to left.
	2		
	3	Step back on right.	Step back on left.
	4		
3	1 ⎫		
	2 ⎬ Contretemps back.	Contretemps back.	
	3 ⎪ (Hop on right.)	(Hop on left.)	
	4 ⎭		
4	1	Assemblé, left to first position.	Assemblé, right to first position.
	2		
	3	Pause.	Pause.
	4		

La Gavotte du Roi. (Figure II.).

Bar.	Beat.	Gentlemen.	Ladies.
B. 1	1 ⎫		
	2 ⎬ Contretemps forward.		
	3 ⎪ (Hop on right.)		
	4 ⎭		
		The two gentlemen meet and pass right shoulders.	
2	1	Assemblé, left to first position. On the Assemblé both gentlemen make a half turn right, and face each other in opposite places.	The ladies wait for two bars.
	2		
	3	Step back on right.	
	4		

151

Bar.	Beat.	Gentlemen.	Ladies.
B. 3	1	Contretemps back. (Hop on right.)	Contretemps forward (hop on right), to meet and pass right shoulders.
	2		
	3		
	4		
4	1	Assemblé, left to first position.	Assemblé, left to first position, making half turn to face each other.
	2		
	3	Pause.	Step back on right.
	4		
5	1		
	2		Contretemps back. (Hop on right.)
	3		
	4	Wait two bars.	
6	1		Assemblé left to first position.
	2		
	3		
	4		Pause.

LA GAVOTTE DU ROI. (Figure III.).

Bar.	Beat.	Gentlemen.	Ladies.
C. 1	1		
	2	Contretemps forward to centre. (Hop on left.)	Contretemps forward to centre. (Hop on left.)
	3		
	4		
2	1	Assemblé, right to first position.	Assemblé, right to first position.
	2		
	3	Step back on left, one-eighth turn right.	Step back on left, one-eighth turn right.
	4		
3	1		
	2	Contretemps back to centre sides. (Hop on left.)	Contretemps back, one to top, one to bottom. (Hop on left.)
	3		
	4		
4	1	Assemblé, right to first position.	Assemblé, right to first position.
	2		
	3	Pause.	Pause.
	4		

La Gavotte du Roi. (Figure IV.).

C. 2.

Bar.	Beat.	Gentlemen.	Ladies.
1	1 2 3 4	Contretemps forward diagonally. (Hop on right.)	Contretemps forward diagonally. (Hop on right.)
2	1	Assemblé, left to first position, making quarter turn to face centre.	Assemblé, left to first position, making quarter turn to face centre.
	2		
	3	Pause.	Pause.
	4		
3	1 2 3 4	Contretemps back. (Hop on left.)	Contretemps back. (Hop on left.)
4	1	Assemblé right to first position.	Assemblé right to first position.
	2		
	3	Pause.	Pause.
	4		

La Gavotte du Roi. (Figure V.).

D. (= B.).

Bar.	Beat.	Gentlemen.	Ladies.
1	1 2 3 4	Contretemps to centre. (Hop on right.)	Quarter turn left. Contretemps to corner. (Hop on left.)
2	1 2 3 4	Assemblé, left to first position, half turn to face partner.	Assemblé, right to first position. Quarter turn right to face partner.
3	1 2 3 4	Contretemps. (Hop on left, half turn right), go to centre top (or bottom) to meet the contrary lady.	Contretemps. (Hop on left, half turn right), go to centre top (or bottom) to meet the contrary gentleman.

153

D. (= B.).

Bar.	Beat.	Gentlemen.	Ladies.
4	1	Assemblé, right to first position,	Assemblé, right to first position
	2	three-quarter turn to right.	turning to face the contrary
	3		gentleman.
	4	Pause.	Step back on left.
5	1		
	2	Contretemps back.	Contretemps back.
	3	(Hop on left.)	(Hop on left.)
	4		
6	1	Assemblé, right to first position.	Assemblé, right to first position.
	2		
	3	Pause.	Pause.
	4		

Dezais' Diagram does not make it clear that the contrary ladies and gentlemen meet in the *centre* (top and bottom) in the 3rd bar, but this must be intended because in bar 5 they withdraw equally to corners.

LA GAVOTTE DU ROI. (Figure VI.).

E. (= C.).

Bar.	Beat.	Gentlemen.	Ladies.
1	1	Contretemps. (Hop on the right,	Contretemps forward to original
	2	quarter turn left on the hop.)	place. (Hop on right.)
	3	Follow partner round in a	
	4	circle.	
2	1	Assemblé, left to first position,	Assemblé, left to first position
	2	quarter turn right.	quarter turn right.
	3		
	4	Step back on right.	Step back on right.
3	1		
	2	Contretemps back. (Hop on	Contretemps back. (Hop on
	3	right.)	right.)
	4		
4	1	Assemblé, left to first position.	Assemblé, left to first position.
	2		
	3	Pause.	Pause.
	4		

The dancers are now in their original places, but the ladies on the wrong side of their partners. The next figure puts them right.

LA GAVOTTE DU ROI. (Figure VII.).

E. 2 (C = 2).

Bar.	Beat.	Gentlemen.	Ladies.
1	1 2 3 4	Contretemps. (Hop on left, quarter turn left.)	Contretemps. (Hop on right, quarter turn right.)
2	1 2 3 4	Assemblé, left to first position, half turn right. Pause.	Assemblé, right to first position. Pause.
3	1 2 3 4	Contretemps back. (Hop on left.)	Contretemps back. (Hop on right.)
4	1 2 3 4	Demi-coupé right. Slide the left to fourth position behind, on the toes. Lower the heels.	Demi-coupé left. Slide the right to fourth position behind, on the toes. Lower the heels.

The weight is on the rear foot (outside), leaving inside feet pointed in front. Now, without any music, repeat the Honours made at the beginning of the dance.

THE COTILLON.

The Eighteenth-century Cotillon was always a square dance for eight people : it began with the Grand Rond, and consisted of several figures linked by one or other of the movements called " Changes." Perhaps the most popular Change was that called " La Course," or the Promenade.

It was usual for a figure to be danced by the first and third couples, and then repeated for the second and fourth couples. This repetition gave the Cotillon its alternative name of Contredanse or Counter-dance. In England the repetition was called the Counter-part. It is important to remember this because many people still imagine that Contredanse is a bad French translation of Country Dance ; or even that our Country Dance is not English at all, but a poor copy of the French.

The steps to be used in Cotillons were seldom indicated, the dancer being allowed freedom of choice ; but in practice the music or the nature of the figure will decide this question.

Figure dancing demands simple steps, and the three in general use were the Chassé, the Contretemps, and the Rigadoon. The Chassé is most comfortable where the music is in 6/8 time, and there is a lot of ground to be covered.

Chassé to the left. Stand in the second position, with the weight on the left foot, raise the right foot to the side.

Bar.	Beat.	
1	1	Bring the right foot sharply to the first position, and raise the left to the side.
	2	
	3	Step on the left in second position.
	4	Bring the right foot sharply to the first position, and raise the left to the side.
	5	
	6	Step on the left in second position.

The English name for this step was the Drive, because the right foot drives the left onwards each time.

To Chassé to the right, reverse the feet.

The Chassé forward is done by raising one foot backwards and driving the other forward to the fourth position.

To Chassé back, raise one foot forward and drive the other back to the fourth position behind.

Chassés should be performed very smoothly, and close to the ground ; the weight must be kept well forward over the advancing foot.

The Contretemps. This step is usually best with 2/4 or 4/4 time.

Bar.	Beat.	
1	1	Hop on the left foot and advance the right.
	2	Step forward on the right foot.
	3	Step forward on the left foot.
	4	

The hop must be small, and the weight well forward over the advancing foot. The general effect should be of a brisk trot.

Where several Contretemps are made in succession, they will begin with the same foot. Contretemps may be made with either foot ; forward, back or turning. They are not usually made to the side.

A run of Chassés or Contretemps was generally finished with an Assemblé.

This means that instead of making the last step of the Contretemps to the fourth position, the foot is brought to the first position with a little spring on both feet.

In a run of Chassés the last one must be sacrificed, and instead of driving with the rear foot, it is brought to the first position with a little spring.

Since the first position is neutral, it is possible to begin again with either foot and in any direction.

The Pas de Rigadoon was made in place, and began from the first position. Stand with the weight on the left foot.

Bar. Beat.

1 1 Hop on the left foot, raising the right to the side.

   2 Bring the right foot sharply to the first position, raising the left to the side.

" and " Return the left foot to first position.

   3 Make a small spring on both feet.

   4

Pas de Rigadoon may also be made with the contrary feet.

The Balancé, also made in place, is the English Country Dance " Setting " performed with rather more finish.

Bar. Beat.

   6 Bend both knees and slide the left foot to the second position.

1 1 Rise on the toes of the left foot and close the right to first.

   2 Lower the heels.

   3 Bend both knees and slide the right foot to second position.

   4 Rise on the toes of the right foot, closing left to first position.

   5 Lower the heels.

   6

The Bow and Curtsy before the Cotillon will be the same that were used for the Gavotte. See p. 131.

In the Nineteenth Century the Cotillon changed its form entirely and became a kind of dancing game, in which the figures were competitions with prizes for the winners. The prizes were by no means awarded for the best dancing, since the actual competitions were often of a ridiculous nature with the dance as a finale.

EXAMPLE XXI (*a*)
(Music : p. 161.)

I. " LES FLEURS DU PRINTEMS "

Cotillon, selected from the Collection given by Giovanni Gallini in " Critical Observations on the Art of Dancing." (1770.)

157

LE GRAND ROND.

Bar. Beat.

A. 1   1 Drive with the right foot.

      2   } Chassé.

      3 Step on the left in second position.

      4 Drive with the right foot.

      5   } Chassé.

      6 Step on the left in second position.

  2   1

      2 } Chassé.

      3

      4

      5 } Chassé.

      6

  3   1

      2 } Chassé.

      3

      4

      5 } Chassé.

      6

  4   1

      2 } Chassé.

      3

      4

      5 } Chassé.

      6

  5   1

      2 } Chassé.

      3

      4

      5 } Chassé.

      6

  6   1

      2 } Chassé.

      3

      4

      5 } Chassé.

      6

  7   1

      2 } Chassé.

      3

      4

      5 } Chassé.

      6

  8   1

      2 } Chassé.

      3

All eight dancers take hands in a ring, which must be as large as possible to ensure firmness. In this position they make 15 Chassés to the left, and finish with an Assemblé.

A. 1. *Beat.*

4 ⎫ Close the right foot in first position
5 ⎬ with a   ⎫ Assemblé.
6 ⎭ Small spring on both feet.   ⎭

A. 2.

Repeat the above, moving round by the right to places.

Bar. Beat.

B.   First and Third Couples.

Bar	Beat			
	6	Raise the right foot backwards.		First and Third
1	1	Drive with the right foot.	Chassé.	Couples meet and take both hands with the person opposite.
	2			
	3	Step forward on the left.	Chassé.	
	4	Drive with the right foot.		
	5			
	6	Step forward on the left.		
2	1	Drive with the right foot sideways.	Chassé.	They change places, moving round to the left.
	2			
	3	Step with the left to second position.	Chassé.	
	4	Drive with the right foot sideways.		
	5			
	6	Step with the left to second position.		
3	1	Drive with the right foot sideways.	Chassé.	
	2			
	3	Step with the left to second position.	Chassé.	
	4	Drive with the right foot backwards.		Release hands and fall back into opposite places.
	5			
	6	Step back with the left foot.		
4	1	Drive with the right foot backwards.		
	2	Step back with the left foot.		
	3		Assemblé.	
	4	Close the right foot to first position.		
	5			
	6	Spring with both feet in first position.		

Bars 5 to 8, the Second and Fourth Couples do the same. All are now in the opposite places.

B. Repeated.

Bar. Beat.

Bar	Beat		
1	1	Drive with the left foot.	} Chassé.
	2		
	3	Step forward with the right.	
	4	Drive with the left foot.	} Chassé.
	5		
	6	Step forward with the right.	
2	1	} Chassé.	
	2		
	3		
	4	} Chassé.	
	5		
	6		
3	1	} Chassé.	
	2		
	3		
	4	} Chassé.	
	5		
	6		
4	1	} Chassé.	
	2		
	3		
	4	} Chassé.	
	5		
	6		
5	1	} Chassé.	
	2		
	3		
	4	} Chassé.	
	5		
	6		
6	1	} Chassé.	
	2		
	3		
	4	} Chassé.	
	5		
	6		
7	1	} Chassé.	
	2		
	3		
	4	} Chassé.	
	5		
	6		
8	1	} Chassé.	
	2		
	3		
	4	} Chassé.	
	5		
	6		

All eight meet with 2 chassés and give right hands across; they move half way round, to reach their original places (4 chassés).

Then release hands and spread towards their own places (2 chassés).

The ladies are on the wrong side of their partners.

Partners give right hands (2 chassés), and make a half turn in their own places to reach the correct side (4 chassés).

Release hands.
The lady must finish with a half turn right, to face the centre (2 chassés).

160

COTILLON
"Les Fleurs du Printems"
Gallini. Original Harmonies

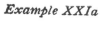

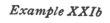

Example XXIb

COTILLON
"La Tirolaise"
Gallini. Original Harmonies

EXAMPLE XXI (b)

II. " LA TIROLAISE "

COTILLON. (GALLINI. 1770.)

Since this dance is used as a second figure, instead of " Le Grand Rond " a Change is used ; in this case it is a form of " La Course," otherwise called " La Promenade."

Bar. Beat.

A. 1   1
        2 } The lady is, as usual, on her partner's right. They take hands
        3 crossed in front ; that is to say, each gentleman with his right
        4 hand takes the lady's right hand, and with his left hand, her left.
        5 (Figure XXII (*e*) 6.).
        6

2   1
        2
        3 } In this position they all move round to the right, moving briskly and
        4 lightly with two walking steps to the bar.
        5
        6

3   1
        2
        3
        4
        5
        6 } By the fourth bar, each couple has moved to the place of the next,
4   1 and all face the centre.
        2
        3
        4
        5
        6

For Bars 5 to 8 continue in the same way. By the eighth bar they will all be the opposite places.

" A " is then repeated so that every couple finishes in its original place.

Bar.	Beat.			
B.		First and Third Couples.		
1	1	Hop on the left foot.	⎱	⎫
	2			
	3	Step forward on the right foot.	Contre-	The first and third couples
	4	Step forward on the left foot.	temps.	meet. Each gentleman,
	5			with his left hand, takes
	6			the right hand of the
2	1	Hop on the left foot.	⎱	opposite lady, and raises
	2			it.
	3	Step forward on the right foot.	Contre-	
	4	Step forward on the left foot.	temps.	
	5			
	6		⎰	⎬
3	1	Hop on the left foot.	⎱	
	2			
	3	Step forward on the right foot.	Contre-	
	4	Step forward on the left foot.	temps.	The gentlemen stand still.
	5			The ladies make a turn to
	6			their right, passing under
4	1	Hop on the left foot.	⎱	the gentleman's arm, and
	2			coming in to meet the
	3	Step forward on the right foot.	Contre-	opposite lady.
	4	Step forward on the left foot.	temps.	
	5			
	6		⎰	Release hands.
5	1	Drive with the right foot.	⎱	⎫
	2		Chassé.	
	3	Step forward on the left foot.		
	4	Drive with the right foot.		
	5		Chassé.	
	6	Step forward on the left foot.	⎰	
6	1			
	2	Chassé.		
	3			
	4			
	5	Chassé.		The ladies give left hands
	6			across and the gentlemen
7	1		⎬	do the same. All move
	2	Chassé.		round to the right to their
	3			own places. (Moulinet.)
	4			
	5	Chassé.		
	6			
8	1			
	2	Chassé.		
	3			
	4			
	5	Chassé.		
	6		⎭	

163

B. Repeated.
The same figure danced by the Second and Fourth Couples.

EXAMPLE XXI (c)

III. "LE POUVOIR DE LA BEAUTÉ"

Cotillon. (Gallini. 1770.).

Instead of Le Grand Rond, use another variation of the Promenade.
The lady is on her partner's right. His right hand holds her left.

Bar.	Beat.	
A.	2	Raise the left foot backwards.
1	1	Drive with the left foot, step forward on right = Chassé. ⎫ All move round one place.
	2	Drive with the left foot, step forward on right = Chassé.
2	1	Chassé.
	2	Chassé. ⎭
3	1	Chassé. ⎫
	2	Chassé. Still holding hands, the ladies turn to the left under their
4	1	Chassé. partner's arm.
	2	⎭
5	1	Chassé. ⎫
	2	Chassé. All move round one place.
6	1	Chassé.
	2	Chassé. ⎭
7	1	Chassé. ⎫
	2	Chassé. The ladies turn under their partner's arm as before.
8	1	Chassé. All are now in the opposite places.
	2	Chassé. ⎭

A. Repeated.

Continue as above to original places.

B.

		First and Third Couples.	*Second and Fourth Couples.*
1	1	Chassé. ⎫ Change with opposites,	Drive with left step ⎫ Slow
	2	Chassé. giving right hands in	forward right. ⎭ Chassé.
2	1	Chassé. passing.	
	2	Chassé. ⎭	Chassé. ⎫
3	1	Chassé. ⎫	Chassé.
	2	Chassé. Partners change, giving	Allemande with four
4	1	Chassé. left hands in passing.	Chassé. slow Chassés.
	2	Chassé. ⎭	
5	1	Chassé. ⎫	Chassé. ⎭
	2		Chassé. ⎫
6	1	Chassé.	Chassé. Change with opposites,
	2	Allemande with four	Chassé. giving right hands in
7	1	Chassé. slow Chassés.	Chassé. passing.
	2		Chassé. Partners change, giving
8	1	Chassé. ⎭	Chassé. left hands in passing.
	2		Chassé. ⎭

Example XXIc

COTILLON
"Le Pouvoir de la Beauté"
Gallini. Original Harmonies

A.

All are now in the opposite places.

> Bars 1-4. Continuing with the same Chassés, all eight give right hands across and move round to the left (clockwise).
>
> Bars 5 and 6. Four Chassés, releasing hands and spreading out towards their own places.
>
> Bars 7 and 8. Four Chassés, making a half turn right to face the centre in their own places.

MINEUR.

C. Eight bars.

Partners face each other and give right hands in order to commence La Chaine (Hey), four changes giving right and left hands alternately, which will take them half way round to opposite places. Sixteen Chassés, four to each change. Partners have met, and stand facing each other.

C. REPEATED.

Bar.	Beat.		
	2	Bend both knees, step with left to second position.	⎫
1	1	Rise on toes of left foot, closing right to first position and immediately lowering the heels.	
	2	Bend both knees, step with right to second position.	⎬ Balancé.
2	1	Rise on toes of right foot, closing left to first position and immediately lowering the heels.	
	2		⎭
3	1	Hop on the left, raise right in second position and return it to first.	⎫
	2	Raise the left in second position and return it to first.	⎬ Rigadoon.
4	1	Spring on both feet in first position.	
	2	Raise the left foot backwards.	⎭
5	1	Drive with left, step forward right for Chassé.	⎫
	2	Chassé.	
6	1	Chassé.	Partners put left hand
	2	Chassé.	behind to take part-
7	1	Chassé.	ner's right; and
	2	Chassé.	⎬ Allemande with six
8	1	Spring, with both feet to first position. (Assemblé.)	Chassés.
	2	Disengage the arms, face partner, and give right hand to continue La Chaine.	⎭

D. Bars 1-8. La Chaine as before, half way round to original places; partners meet and face each other.

C. Bars 1-8. Balancé, Rigadoon, and Allemande as above.

EXAMPLE XXII

ALLEMANDE. (Gallini. 1770.)

The Allemande was a square dance for eight, like the Cotillon. Thomas Wilson, writing in the early Nineteenth Century, deplored the confusion that had developed because Cotillons, which should be written in triple time, were also using duple time. Even in 1770 there was considerable laxity in respect of time and of the steps employed. The Cotillon should be written in triple time and the Allemande in duple time.

LE GRAND ROND.

All eight take hands in a ring, which should be stretched firmly as in the Cotillons.

A. ONCE.

All move round to the left with seven Chassés and an Assemblé (for the Chassés, drive with the right and move the left to second position ; for the Assemblé spring with both feet to land in first position).

A. REPEATED.

Reverse the direction and make seven Chassés, driving with the left foot and finishing with an Assemblé in original places.

B.

Bar. Beat.

Bar	Beat			
1	1	Hop on right, step forward with left.	Contretemps.	The first and third couples meet.
	2	Step forward with right.		
2	1	Hop on right, step forward with left.	Contretemps.	
	2	Step forward with right.		
3	1	Drive with left step forward right. Chassé.		Put left hand behind to take right hand of opposite person, and Allemande.
	2	Chassé.		
4	1	Chassé.		
	2	Chassé.		
5	1	Hop on right, step back with left.	Contretemps.	The first and third couples fall back.
	2	Step back with right.		
6	1	Hop on right, step back with left.	Contretemps.	
	2	Step back with right.		
7	1	Drive with left step forward right. Chassé.		The gentlemen make a half turn right. All put left hand behind to take partner's right hand and Allemande. The gentlemen must make another turn to finish facing centre.
	2	Chassé.		
8	1	Chassé.		
	2	Chassé.		

Example XXII

ALLEMANDE
Gallini. Original Harmonies

Example XXIII

LA GRAZIOSETTA
Gallini, c. 1770. Original Harmonies

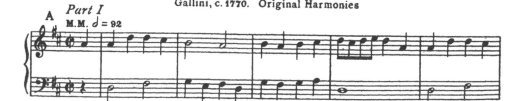

B. Repeated.

The second and fourth couples dance the same figure.

C. Twice Through.

Partners take both hands, crossed behind (Figure XXII (e) 7). The lady puts her right hand behind to take her partner's right. The gentleman puts his left hand behind to take the lady's left. In this position they make the whole Course, turning at each quarter to face the centre.

Four bars of music to each quarter. One Contretemps to every bar, hopping on the right foot. All finish in their original places and release hands.

EXAMPLE XXIII

La Graziosetta. (Gallini. 1770.)

Instead of Le Grand Rond, this dance goes straight into a figure.

Bar.	Beat.		
A. 1	1	Hop on the left foot.	
	2	Step forward on the right.	Contretemps.
	3	Step forward on the left.	
	4		
2	1	Hop on the left foot.	
	2	Step forward on the right.	Contretemps.
	3	Step forward on the left.	
	4		
3	1		
	2	Contretemps.	
	3		
	4		
4	1		
	2	Contretemps.	
	3		
	4		
5	1		
	2	Contretemps.	
	3		
	4		
6	1		
	2	Contretemps.	
	3		
	4		
7	1		
	2	Contretemps.	
	3		
	4		
8	1		
	2	Spring, bringing the right	Assemblé.
	3	foot to first position.	
	4		

The first gentleman, followed by his partner and the second couple, makes a complete circle to the left; whilst the fourth lady, followed by her partner and the third couple, makes a complete circle to the right.

B.

Bar.	Beat.			

I   1   Drive with right foot.   ⎫ Chassé.   ⎫ Partners move to the next place
      2   Step forward on the left. ⎬   ⎬ on their right, and prepare
      3   Drive with right foot.   ⎫ Chassé. ⎭ to Allemande.
      4   Step forward on the left. ⎭

  2   1   Chassé.
      2
      3   Chassé.
      4   Partners Allemande.
  3   1   Chassé.
      2
      3   Chassé.
      4   Partners disengage arms and face each other.

  4   1   Hop on the left foot, raising the right in second position. ⎫
      2   Return right to first position, raising left in second.   ⎪
    and Return left to first position.   ⎬ Rigadoon.
      3   Spring with both feet in first position.   ⎪
      4   Raise the right foot backwards.   ⎭

  5   1   Chassé.
      2   Partners move to the next place on their right, and
      3   Chassé.   prepare to Allemande.
      4
  6   1   Chassé.
      2
      3   Chassé.
      4   Partners Allemande.
  7   1   Chassé.
      2
      3   Chassé.
      4   Partners disengage arms and face each other.

  8   1
      2   Rigadoon.
      3
      4

Bars 9-16. Repeat the steps given above, continuing round to original places.

Note.—Although it is necessary to assign certain bars to certain movements, the figure passes so swiftly from one to another that the dancer must be prepared to anticipate, especially in engaging the arms for the Allemande. It would, in practice, be difficult to say whether the Allemande began with the second Chassé of the first bar or the first Chassé of the second bar.

C.

MINUET.

Bar. Beat.

3 Bend the knees slightly.

1   1 Step forward on the right foot, rising on the toes and closing the left to first position.

  and Lower the heels.

  2 Bend the knees slightly.

  3 Step forward with the left foot, rising on the toes.   } Minuet Step.

2   1 Step forward with the right foot, on the toes.

  2 Step forward with the left foot, on the toes.

  and Lower the heels.

  3 Bend the knees to begin the next step.

3   1

  2

  3 } Minuet Step.

4   1

  2

  3

5   1

  2

  3 } Minuet Step.

6   1

  2

  3

7   1

  2

  3 } Minuet Step.

8   1

  2

  3

With these four Minuet Steps the ladies take hands in the centre and go round to the right; whilst the gentlemen make a circuit to the left outside.

D.

Bar. Beat.

3

1   1

  2 } Minuet Step.

  3

2   1

  2

Partners, holding inside hands, move round to the right into the next place, and take both hands.

3

3   1

  2 } Minuet Step.

  3

4   1

  2

Partners turn round to the right, holding both hands; then the gentleman releases the lady's right hand in order to continue as before.

172

D.

Bar.	Beat.		
5	3 1		
	2 3	} Minuet Step.	Partners, holding inside hands, move round to the right into the next place and take both hands.
6	1 2		
7	3 1		
	2 3	} Minuet Step.	Partners turn round to the right, holding both hands; then the gentleman releases the lady's right hand in order to continue as before.
8	1 2 3		

NOTE.—Here also the figure must flow. At the end of the first Minuet Step partners must be working round to face each other and to take both hands. Even whilst they are going round with the second Minuet Step, they must be preparing to release one hand, and to be in the correct place for the forward movement which follows.

EXAMPLE XXIV

"MY GRANDMOTHER."

By the end of the Eighteenth Century a "Country Dance" meant Longways for as many as will; the other forms were no longer used.

Bows and curtsies were formal at the beginning and end of a dance, but were much simpler than they had been previously. It was usual to play the first eight bars of the dance air before beginning the dance, and in these eight bars the dancers made their bow and curtsy first to the "Presence"—which meant the important people sitting at the top of the room—and then to each other.

Bow.

The gentleman should make a small step to second position with either foot, then close the other to third position in front making a little bow from the waist. He will straighten himself more or less slowly according to the importance of the occasion. Beginning a Country Dance was not an important occasion unless it happened to be at Court.

Curtsy.

The lady would be dressed in Empire style, a short-waisted muslin dress hanging in straight folds to look narrow. She will point one foot in front, keeping her weight on the foot which is behind, and bend the supporting knee. She makes only a slight inclination with her head and shoulders because she should be able to look at the person to whom she curtsies. She, also, will rise more or less slowly, according to the occasion.

173

Example XXIV

Air "Nancy Dawson" to be used for the Country Dance
"MY GRANDMOTHER"

From Thomas Wilson "Companion to the Ballroom"   Arranged by Elsie Palmer

A1 & 2

B

At the end of the Eighteenth Century they were not particular about dancing a dance to its own air, and we are using one called " Nancy Dawson " because it is in 6/8 time which is good for skipping. It was not laid down what step should be used, but the figure of " My Grandmother " depends on moving smoothly, and covering the ground quickly, and skipping is best for the purpose. Step on the crotchets and hop on the quavers, and you will make two skips to each bar. Make small steps and only little hops, because the effect depends on keeping the dance neat.

" My Grandmother." (From " The Lady's View and Pocket Magazine." 1795.)

		Bar.	
A.	1		
	2		Light skipping steps. The first couple turn out, each to their own
	3		side, and come in to meet between the second and third couples.
	4		They take both hands.
	5		Eight skipping steps. The first couple skip round to places.
	6		When they have completed the circle they must release hands and
	7		finish each on their own side facing up.
	8		

A. 2.	1	
	2	
	3	The first couple repeat everything they did in the first eight bars ;
	4	but this time they turn out between the second and third couples
	5	and come in between the third and fourth.
	6	When they finish facing up, this time they hold inside hands.
	7	
	8	

B.	1	Sixteen skipping steps. The first couple skip up to the top of the
	2	dance, release hands, turn out each to their own side and skip
	3	down to the bottom outside the lines.
	4	
	5	
	6	The second couple will become top, and when the music begins again
	7	they will do as the first couple did. So in time every couple comes
	8	to the top and dances down to the bottom.

ALFORD, VIOLET. " The Farandole," in *Journal of the English Folk Dance and Song Society.* Vol. I, No. 1. 1932.

ANGLÈS, HIGINIO. *La Musica en la Corte des Reyes Católicos.*

ARENA, ANTOINE. *Ad Suos Compagnones, etc. C.* 1531.

AUBRY, PIERRE. " Estampies et Danses Reales," in *Le Mercure Musicale.* September, 1906.

BARNARD, E. A. B. *A Seventeenth Century Country Gentleman, 1640-1680.* (Heffer : Cambridge.) 1944.

BERTONI, GIULIO. *La Biblioteca Estense e la Coltura Ferrarese, 1471-1505.* (Torino : E. Loescher.) 1903.

BLADÉ, J. F. *Poésies Populaires de la Gascogne.* 1882.

BOCCACCIO. *Decamerone, 1348.* Ed. Maghiri. (Firenze.) 1827.

BRIFFAULT, ROBERT. *Les Troubadors et le Sentiment Romanesque.* Les Editions du Chêne. (16, Place Vendôme, Paris.) 1945.

CAMBRIDGE MEDIÆVAL HISTORY.

CAROSO, FABRITIO. *Il Ballarino.* (Venice.) 1581.

CAROSO, FABRITIO. *Nobilità di Dame.* (Venice.) 1600.

CHRISTINE DE PISAN. *Le Livre du Duc de Vrais Amans. C.* 1404.

CLOSSON, E. *Le Manuscrit dit des Basses Danses.* De la Bibliothèque de Bourgogne. (Brussels : Lamertin.) 1913.

COUSSEMAKER, C. E. H. *Histoire de l'Harmonie au Moyen Age.* 1852.

COUSSEMAKER, C. E. H. *L'Art Harmonique au XII et XIII Siècles.* 1865.

DANIEL, SAMUEL. *The Vision of Twelve Goddesses : A Royall Masque.* Ed. with Notes by Ernest Law. (Quaritch.) 1880.

DAVIES, SIR JOHN. *Orchestra : A Poem of Dancing.* Ed. E. W. M. Tillyard. (Chatto & Windus.) 1945.

DEZAIS, MR. *Recueil de Danses pour l'Annee.* 1716.

EARLY ENGLISH HARMONY. *Plainsong and Mediæval Music Society.* Vol. II. (Instrumental Dances from B.M. MS Harley 978. Transcribed by Dom Anselm Hughes, O.S.B.).

ELYOT, SIR THOMAS. *The Boke Named the Governour, 1531.* Everyman's Library. (Dent.) 1907.

ELYOT, SIR THOMAS. *The Castel of Helth.* 1534.

ENCYCLOPÆDIA ITALIANA. Article " Danza."

ESSEX, JOHN. *For the Further Improvement of Dancing.* 1710.

FROISSART. *Chronicles.*

GALLAY, J. *Le Mariage de la Musique avec la Danse, 1664.* Published with an Introduction by J. Gallay. (Paris.: Librarie des Bibliophiles.) 1870.
GALLINI, GIOVANNI. *Critical Observations on the Art of Dancing.* (London.) *C.* 1770.
GENNRICH, FRIEDRICH. *Rondeaux, Virelais und Balladen.* Two Vols. I : 1921. II : 1927.

LAUZE, F. DE. *Apologie de la Danse.* 1623.

MSS. SIXTEENTH CENTURY ENGLISH :
 Oxford : Bodleian. Douce. 280.
 Oxford : Bodleian. Rawl. Poet. 108.
 London : B.M. Harl. 367.
FIFTEENTH CENTURY ENGLISH :
 Basse Dances written on Fly Leaf of late Fifteenth Century Catholicon. Salisbury Cathedral Library.
FIFTEENTH CENTURY FRENCH :
 Basse Dances on Fly Leaf of Fifteenth Century MS. *Chronique de France.* Paris Bib. Nat. (Fonds : Fr. 5699. Fol. I, v.)
FIFTEENTH CENTURY ITALIAN :
 CORNAZZANO, ANTONIO. *Libro Dell'arte del Danzare.*
 Rome : Vatican. Capponiano. 203.
 De Arte Saltandi et Choreas Ducendi. Paris Bib. Nat. (Fonds : It. 982.)
 GUGLIELMO HEBRAEI. *Pisauriensis de Pratica seu arte Tripudii Vulghare Opusculum.* (Firenze.) Magliabechiana. (Class XIX. 9. 88.)

NICHOLS, J. *Progresses of Queen Elizabeth.* 1823, 1828.

PEMBERTON, E. *An Essay for the Further Improvement of Dancing, 1711.*
PEPYS, SAMUEL. *Diary.* Ed. Lord Braybrooke. (Simpkin Marshall : London 1.)
PLAYFORD, JOHN. *The English Dancing-Master, 1651.*

RAMEAU, P. *The Dancing-Master.* Trans. C. W. Beaumont from the Original Edition, 1725. (London : C. W. Beaumont.) 1931.

THOINOT, ARBEAU. *Orchesography.* Trans. C. W. Beaumont. (London.) 1925.

SOLERTI, ANGELO. *Ferra e la Corte Estense Nella Seconda Metà del Secolo Decimosesta : I Discorsi di Annibale Romei. Citta di Castello.* 1900.

WILSON, THOMAS. *A Companion to the Ballroom.* 1816.

A FEW BOOKS, MORE READILY OBTAINABLE, SUGGESTED FOR "BACKGROUND" READING

ADDISON, JOSEPH. *Essays*. Ed. J. R. Green. (Macmillan : London.) 1892.

BYRNE, M. ST. CLARE. *The Elizabethan Home*. Extracts from Hollyband and Erondel. Etchells and MacDonald. (London.) 1925.

BYRNE, M. ST. CLARE. *Elizabethan Life in Town and Country*. (Methuen.) 1925.

CARTWRIGHT, JULIA. *Beatrice d'Este*. (Dent.) 1899.

CARTWRIGHT, JULIA. *Isabella d'Este, 1474-1539*. 2 vols. (John Murray : London.) 1903.

CASA, GIOVANNI DE LA. *Galateo*. Trans. Published by J. Dodsley. (London.) 1774.

CASTIGLIONE, BALDASSARE. *Il Cortegiano, 1528*. Trans. as *The Book of the Courtier* by Sir Thomas Hoby. 1561. *Tudor Translations XXIII*. Also in Everyman's Library.

COATE, MARY. *Social Life in Stuart England*. (Methuen.) 1924.

COULTON, G. G. *Life in the Middle Ages*. (Cambridge University Press.) 1929.

CRUMP, LUCY. *Nursery Life 300 Years Ago : The Journals of Dr. Jean Hèroard dealing with the Childhood of Louis XIII and Henrietta Maria*. (Routledge.) 1929.

EVANS, JOAN. *Life in Mediæval France*. (Oxford University Press.) 1925.

GARDINER, DOROTHY. *English Girlhood at School*. (Oxford University Press.) 1929.

HARVEY, JOHN. *The Plantagenets, 1154-1485*. (Batsford.) 1948.

LACROIX. *History of the Masque at the English Court*.

MARCHAND, JEAN. *A Frenchman in England, 1784*. Trans. S. C. Roberts. (Cambridge University Press.) 1933.

PORTER. *Endymion : Life and Letters of*. Ed. Dorothea Townshend. 1897 (Court Life under Charles I.),

POWER, EILEEN. *Le Ménagier de Paris*. Trans. as *The Good Man of Paris* by Eileen Power. (Routledge.) Broadway Mediæval Library.

POWER, EILEEN. *Mediæval People*. Pelican Books. 1937.

SACKVILLE-WEST, V. *Knole and the Sackvilles*.

SACKVILLE-WEST, V. *The Diary of Lady Anne Clifford*. (Heinemann.) 1923.

STUART, D. M. *The Daughters of George III*. (Macmillan.) 1939.

WILSON, DOVER. *Life in Shakespeare's England*. The Cambridge Anthologies. (Cambridge University Press.) 1920.

Also FAMILY CHRONICLES, such as :
The Paston Letters. (Mediæval.)
The Memoirs of the Verney Family. (Seventeenth Century.)

Lightning Source UK Ltd.
Milton Keynes UK
UKOW06f0952200715

255477UK00001B/14/P